Sacred Pelvic Healing Massage
Practice Manual

A Step By Step Guide

by Amara Karuna

Introduction

In a culture where we are shamed around our sexuality and bodies, often we store large amounts of tension, emotions and toxins in our pelvis. This blocks our ability to feel aliveness.

Sacred Pelvic Healing Massage, also called **Sacred Sexual Healing Massage**, was developed by Amara Karuna over years, integrating many styles of pelvic massage bodywork.

This is a unique, slow and penetrating touch on the pelvic area, which most people have never experienced. It is relaxing, nurturing, healing and pleasurable all at once.

This work draws from the techniques of sacred spot massage, Orgasmic Meditation, cranial sacral work, facia release, Rivers of Love bodywork, Chi Nei Tsang, Taoist energy healing and cultivation, and deep tissue and acupressure bodywork.

It integrates an awareness of the sacredness of our bodies and sexual energies, as well as the emotional distresses carried in the pelvic areas. This is very deep work that touches into our core channel energies, and can bring up strong emotions and be very transformative.

It is wonderful for healing any issues around sexuality, shame, or body image and for expanding our capacity for aliveness, pleasure, juiciness and full body orgasms

DEDICATION

For all my loves, and for everyone who dreams of the Divine Beloved

ACKNOWLEDGMENTS

Thanks to all my teachers: Caroline Muir, Joan and Thomas Heartfield, David Bruce Leonard, Saida Desilets, Jerry Brent, Mantak Chia, Bob Orshalom, Minke DeVos. Michael Reed Gach, and many others!

Thanks to my anonymous models for helping create this manual!

---

http://www.karuna-sacredloving.com

for counseling, classes, workshops, writings, videos

Availability and Copyright

Karuna Publishing, PO box 41811, Eugene, OR 97404

sacredloving@mindspring.com

ISBN: 0-9842274-8-2
ISBN-13: 978-0-9842274-8-8

Table of Contents

How to Use This Manual

This is a picture guidebook intended to remind you of the variety of strokes and techniques that you learned in class. Flip through it as you practice with a partner.

There are short descriptions of each move near the images, but the descriptions are not intended to be teaching tools, only as reminders. Use all the moves, or just some of them. This is a suggested progression proven to work well, but you can do them in whatever order feels good. Do each one as many times as you like.

If you would like more instruction in the moves, please purchase a copy of the **training DVD or Video Download, "Sacred Pelvic Healing Massage" from**

www.karuna-sacredloving.com.

It contains a full sequence of the massage treatment that is paced so that you can follow along while you give to someone.

Back Side Massage Strokes

Back Side Strokes

Sacred Pelvic Healing
Massage
Practice Manual
by Amara Karuna ©2016

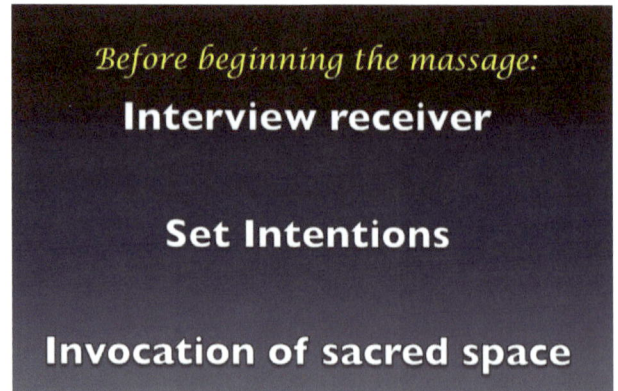
Before beginning the massage:

Interview receiver

Set Intentions

Invocation of sacred space

These strokes are the same on everyone. Find a way to set a sacred space, such as giving chakra blessings, prayers, etc

Ask the receiver about sexual issues, boundaries, fears and requests. Also both state your intention for the session.

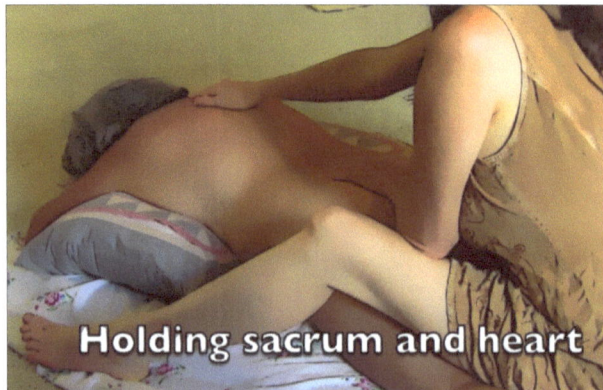
Holding sacrum and heart

Rocking side to side

Take a few breaths as you follow their breathing pattern.

Gentle rocking of the pelvis

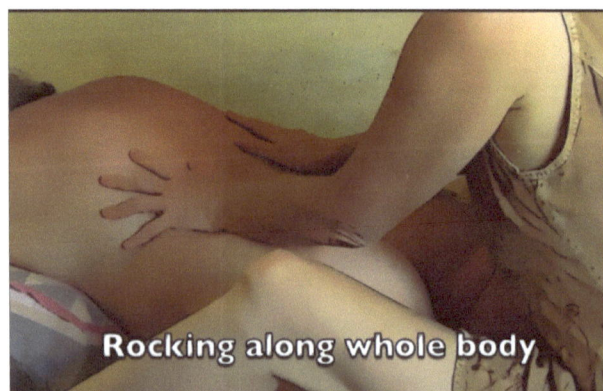
Rocking along whole body

Welcoming full body strokes

Gradually move your hands as you rock

Slow, soft, flowing strokes over whole body

Applying oil slowly

Make the oil application part of the massage

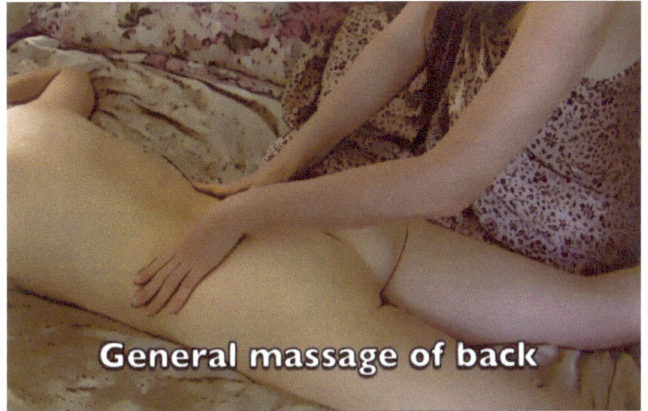

General massage of back

Spend more or less time on the back depending on your time availability

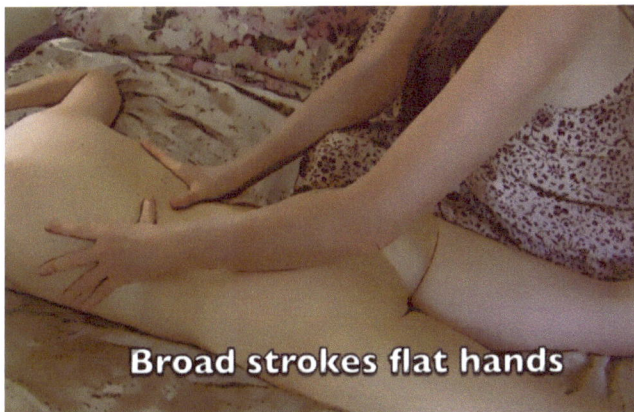

Broad strokes flat hands

Press firmly as you stroke up with broad pressure

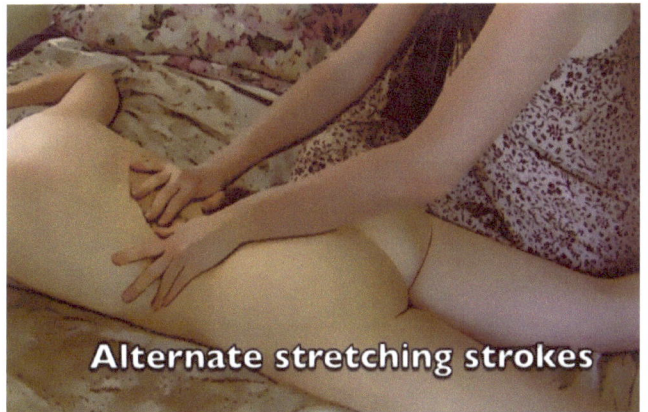

Alternate stretching strokes

Alternate your hands pressing and stretching in arcing movements

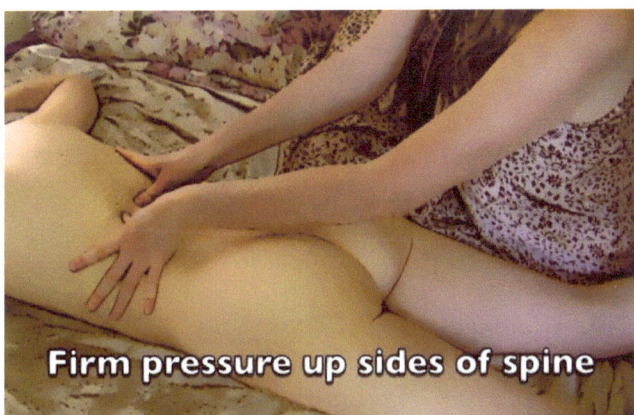

Firm pressure up sides of spine

Pressure points up the spine, right next to the bones. Also long strokes up, then down the sides of body

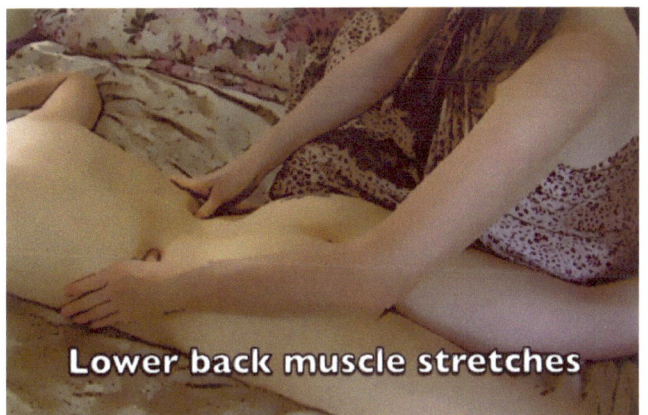

Lower back muscle stretches

Pay attention to the lower one third of the back, between the ribs and sacrum

Pressure circles above boney ridge

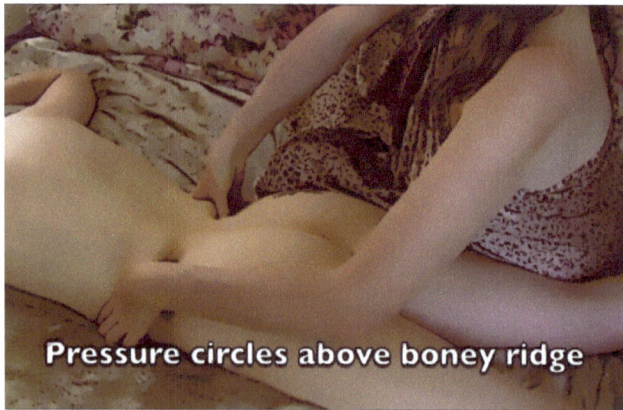

Follow the ridge of the bones of the pelvis, pressing in small circles, starting at spine and moving to hips

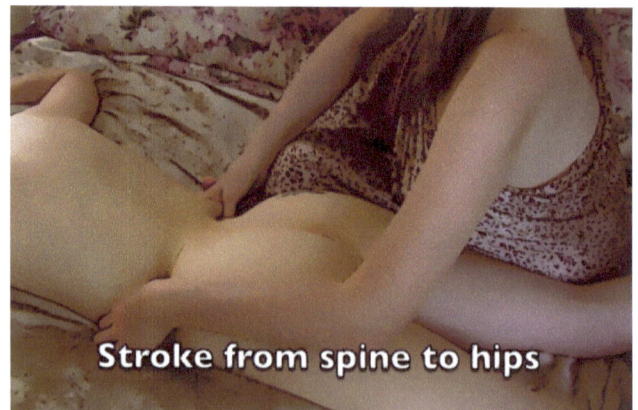

Stroke from spine to hips

Follow the ridge of the bones of the pelvis in a smooth firm stroke from spine to hips

Circles on Hip Bones

Outline the bones of the outsides of the hips with your fingertips in small circles

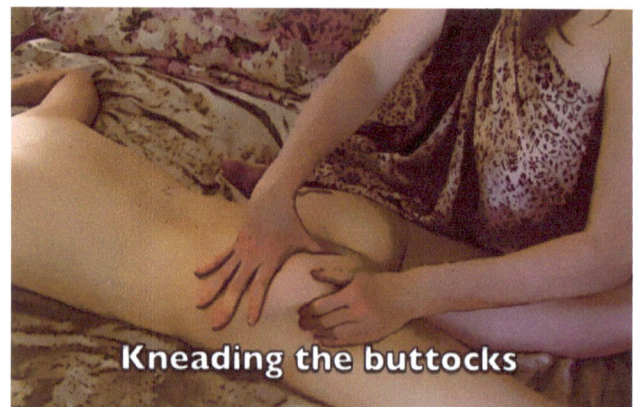

Kneading the buttocks

Knead and squeeze the buttocks... they love it!

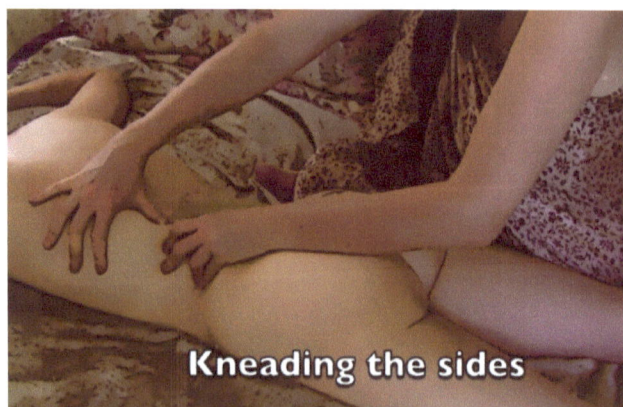

Kneading the sides

Continue the same kneading movement up the sides of the body, more gently

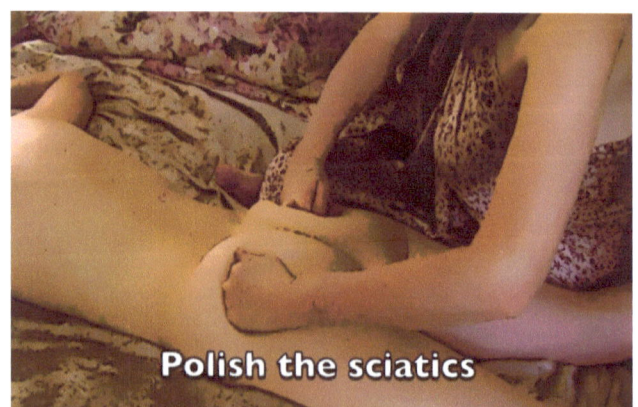

Polish the sciatics

Using fists, press in circles on the sciatic points

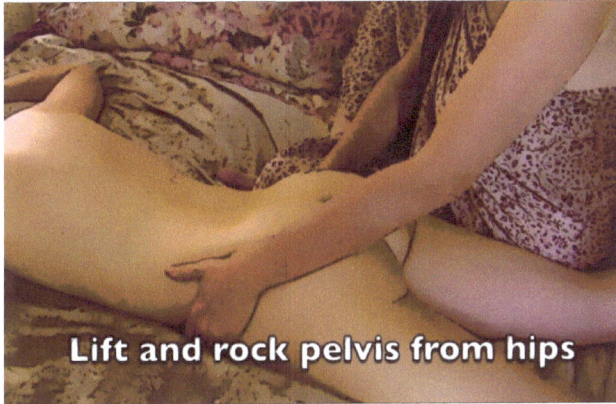

Lift and rock pelvis from hips

With fingers under hip bones, lift the whole pelvis and rock it sideways

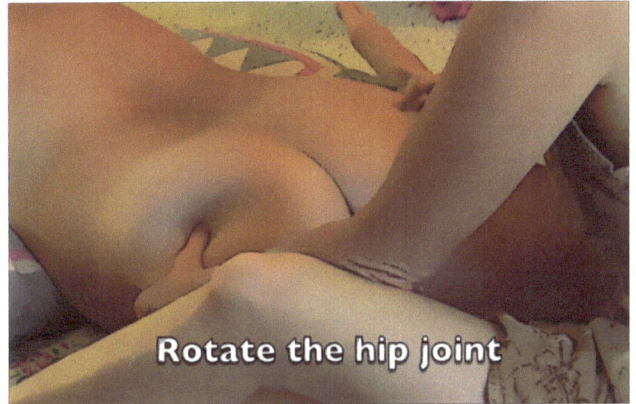

Rotate the hip joint

Find the round bone on the side and move it around, as well as massage around the edges of it

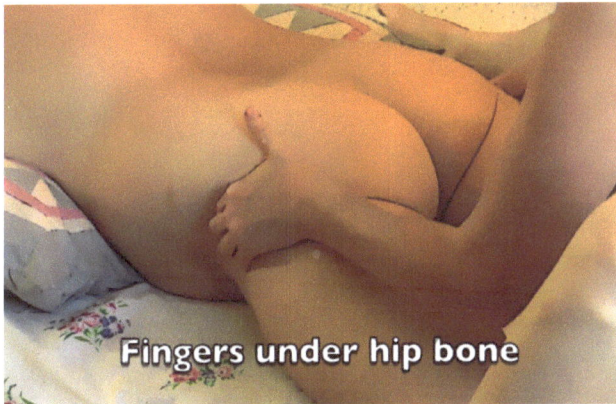

Fingers under hip bone

With fingers under hip bones, massage around the large blade of each hip

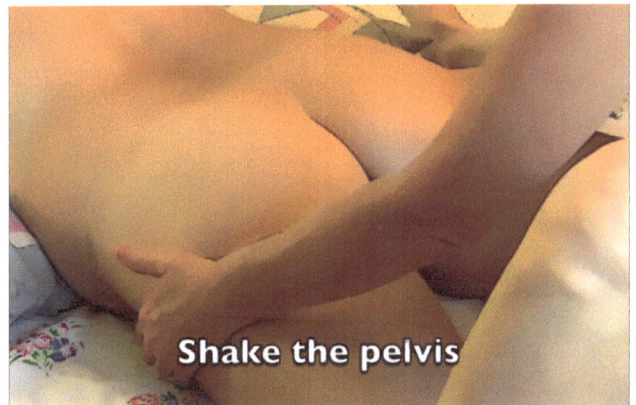

Shake the pelvis

With fingers under hip bones, shake the whole pelvis

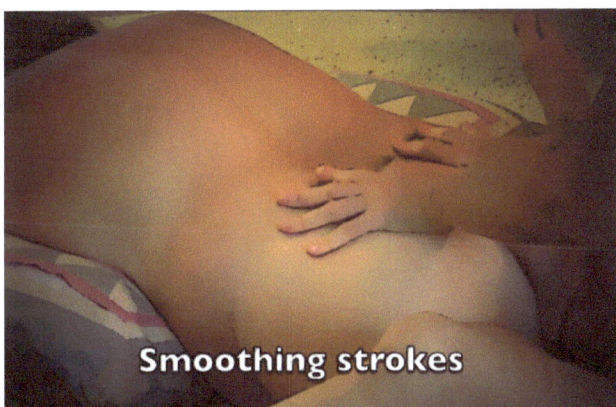

Smoothing strokes

Soft slow strokes on back and buttocks and thighs

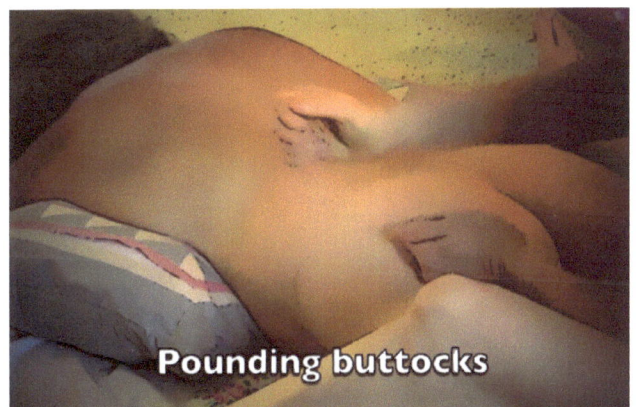

Pounding buttocks

With loose fists, pound firmly and quickly on the buttocks and thighs

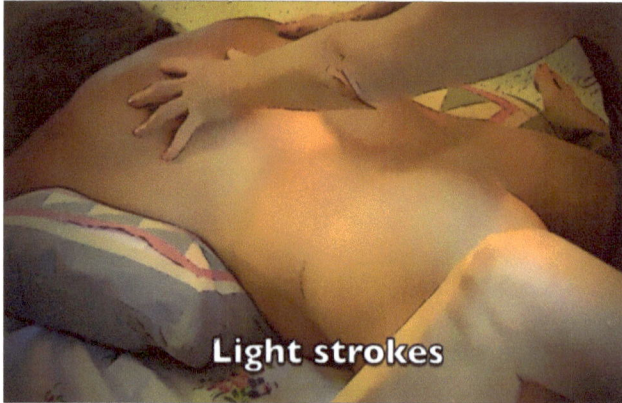

Light strokes

Light fingertip strokes over whole back, slowly

Pressure points on the sacrum

Press deeply on the lines of points on the sacrum, and make small circles while pressing

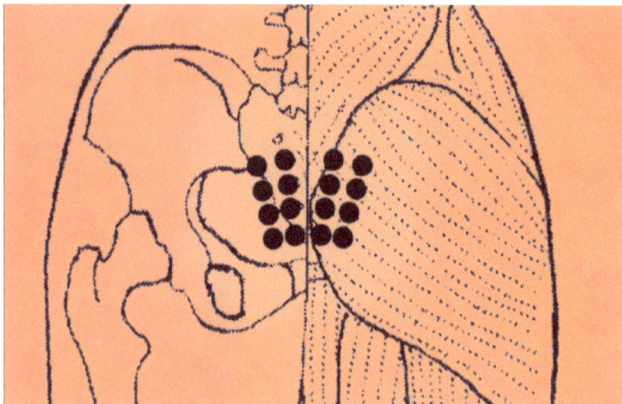

Sacrum points

Image from Acupressure for Lovers

Pressure point circles edge of sacrum

Press deeply on the lines of points on the outside edges of the sacrum, and make small circles while pressing

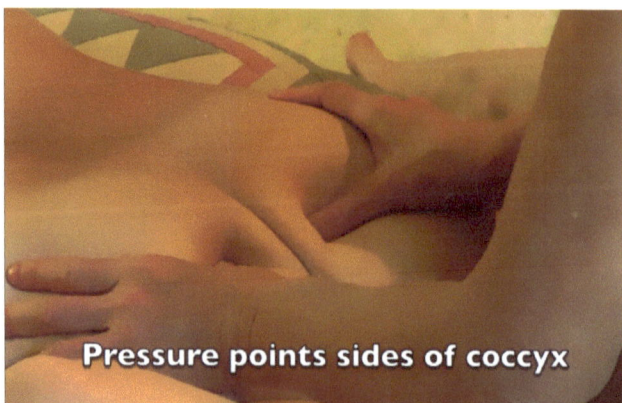

Pressure points sides of coccyx

Continue down the "V" of the sacrum to the sides of the coccyx. Do not press hard directly on it, just to the sides.

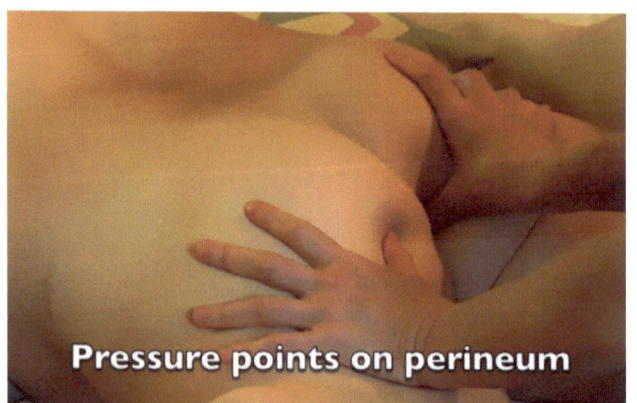

Pressure points on perineum

Press deeply on the line of points going down into the perineum, and make small circles while pressing

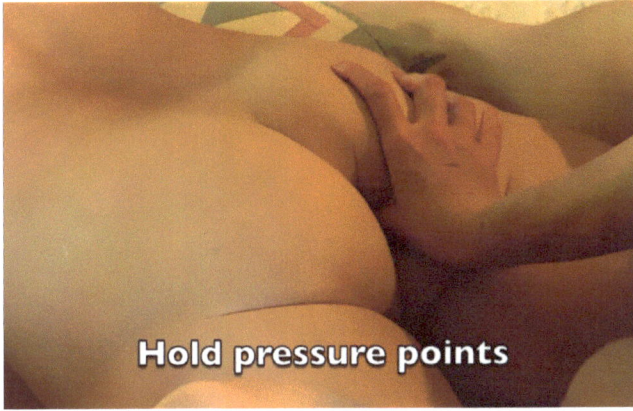

Hold pressure points

Press and hold the perineum points, pushing into the sits bones, and curling around under and inside them

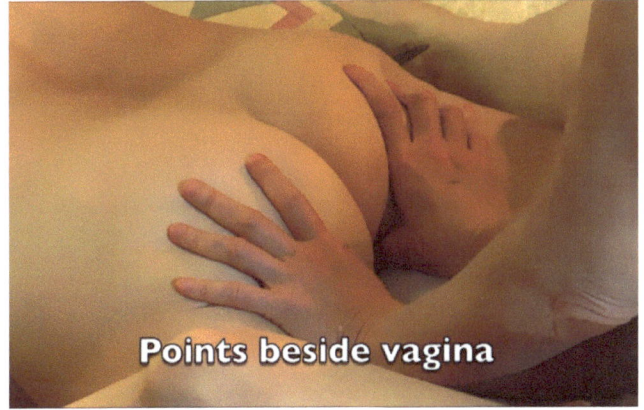

Points beside vagina

Press deeply on the points on the side of the vagina, and make small circles while pressing

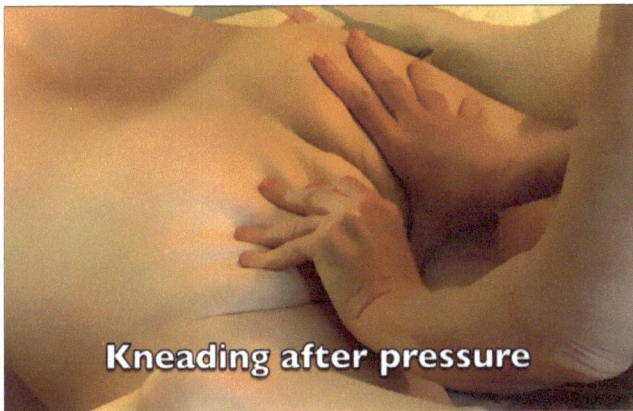

Kneading after pressure

Knead the whole area slowly and gently to spread the energy after the deep pressure points

Pressure points along buttock crease

Press deeply on the line of points in the crease between the buttock and leg, and make small circles from center to sides

Smoothing strokes

Do some full body slow smoothing strokes to finish

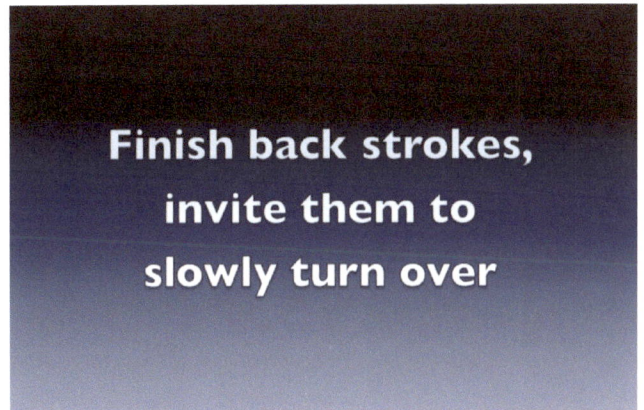

Finish back strokes, invite them to slowly turn over

Decide what position you will work in on the front side and arrange yourselves

Front Side Breast and Yoni Massage

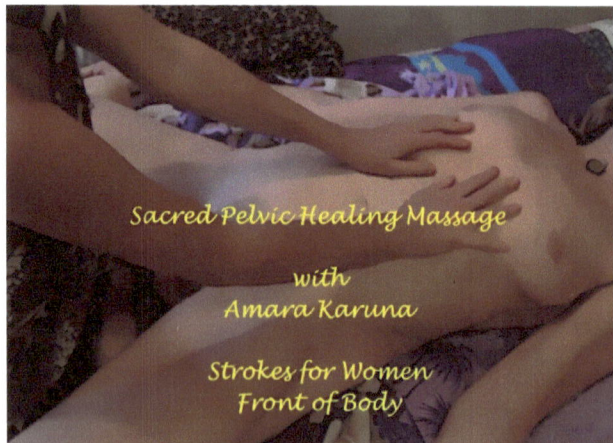

Sacred Pelvic Healing Massage

with
Amara Karuna

Strokes for Women
Front of Body

Work with a woman from the extremities toward the center, working on the yoni last

Hands on yoni and heart

Take a moment to look in her eyes, breathe and connect, after you ask permission to hold her yoni and heart

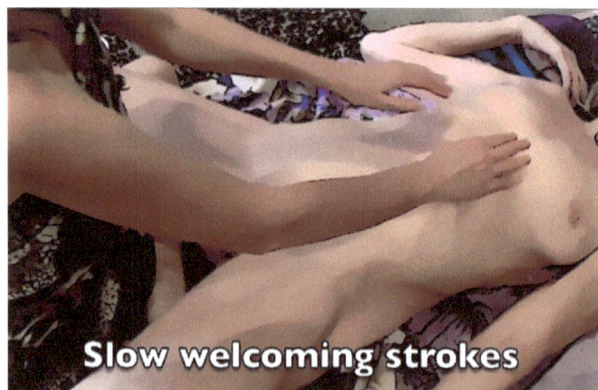

Slow welcoming strokes

Begin with slow, soft sensual strokes over whole body, avoiding the nipples and yoni for now

Applying oil

Apply oil in a slow, flowing manner to torso and breasts but not the yoni

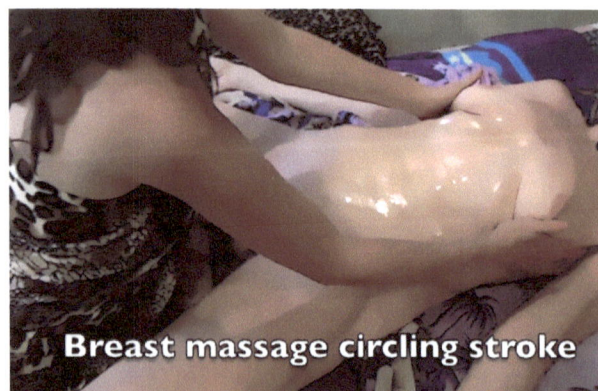

Breast massage circling stroke

Circle each breast with large smooth strokes, going up the middle and down the outsides to flush lymph

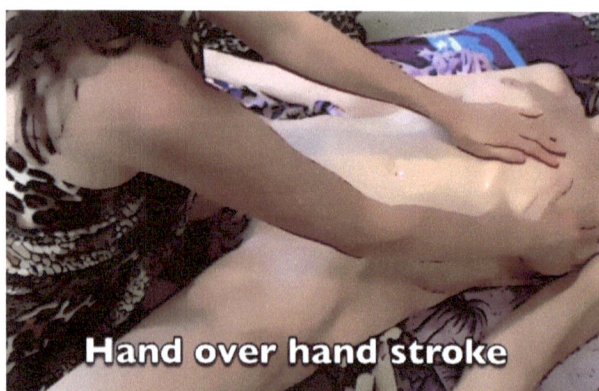

Hand over hand stroke

Using each hand alternately, circle one breast at a time, around the nipple

Pressing from center outward

Starting at one nipple, press firmly to outside of one breast with both hands, used different angles

Spiral small circles around

Using fingertips, move in a spiral around the outside of the breast, pressing gently as you move all the tissue

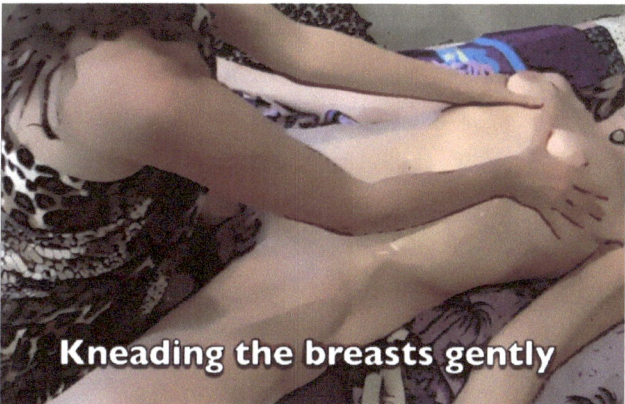

Kneading the breasts gently

Use the whole hand to knead each breast

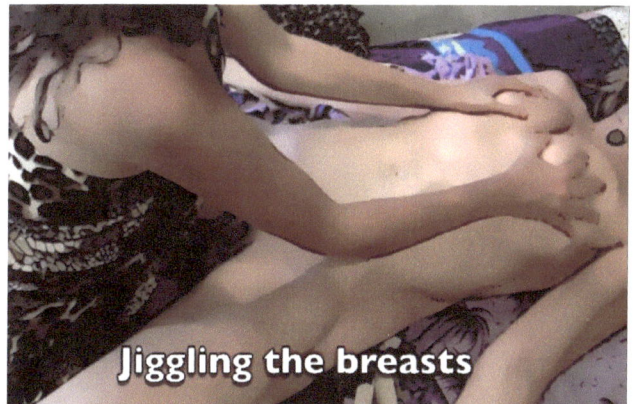

Jiggling the breasts

Press and jiggle each breast

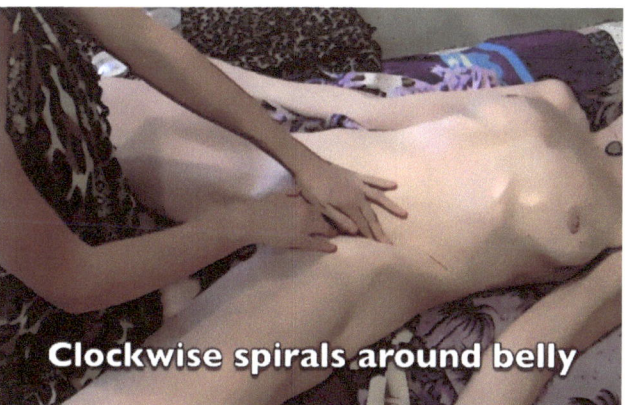

Clockwise spirals around belly

After some **smooth flat hand circles** on belly, move in a clockwise spiral making small circles on the large intestine

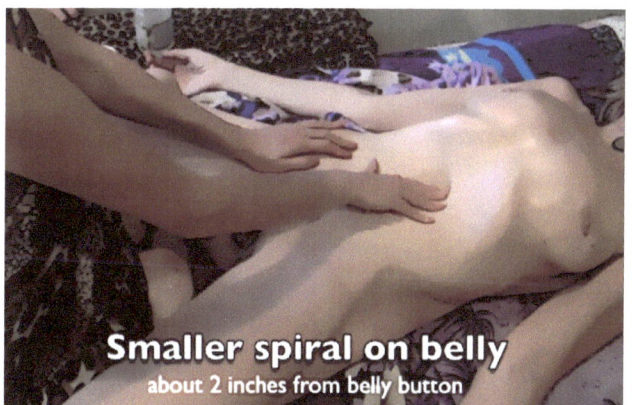

Smaller spiral on belly
about 2 inches from belly button

Move in a smaller clockwise spiral making small circles on the small intestine

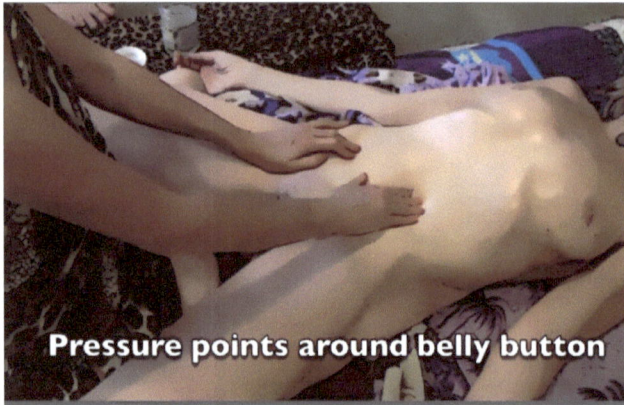

Pressure points around belly button

Pressing deeply a half inch from the belly button, move clockwise making small circles all around it

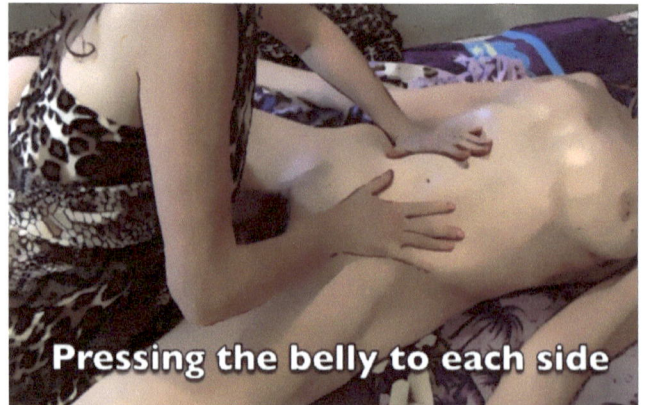

Pressing the belly to each side

With a broad flat hand, lean in from one side to press the whole belly in the opposite direction. Repeat from other side

Sweep from spine over hips
press on pubic bone

Reaching under to touch the sine with your fingertips, press up firmly and sweep around sides, over hips, to press pelvic bone

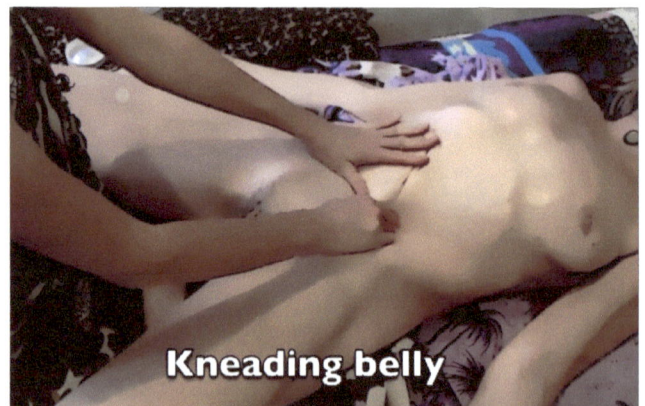

Kneading belly

Knead the whole belly slowly

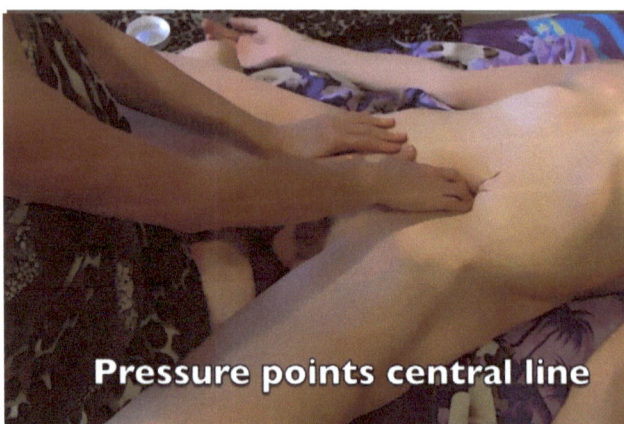

Pressure points central line

Deep pressure on the line of points from the belly button down to pubic bone

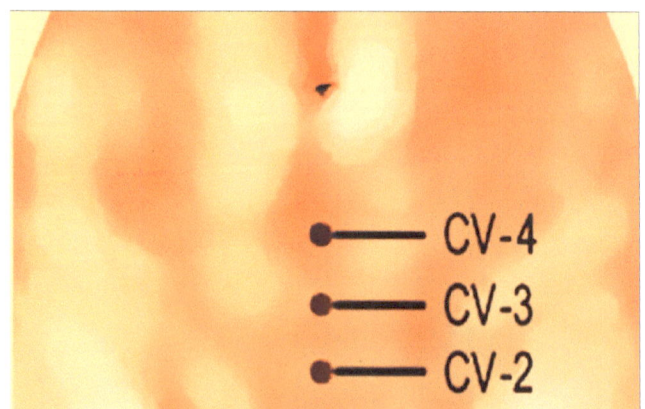

CV-4
CV-3
CV-2

Some of the central points in the "Sea of Intimacy"

Hip and leg connection
focus on wings of the pelvic bone

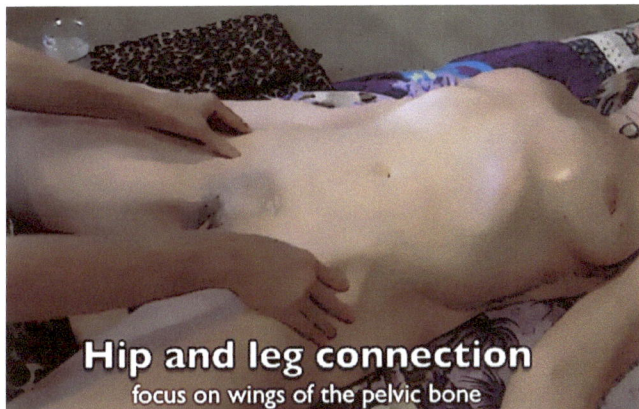

Massage the attachment of the upper thigh muscle to the torso, and around the wings of the hip bones

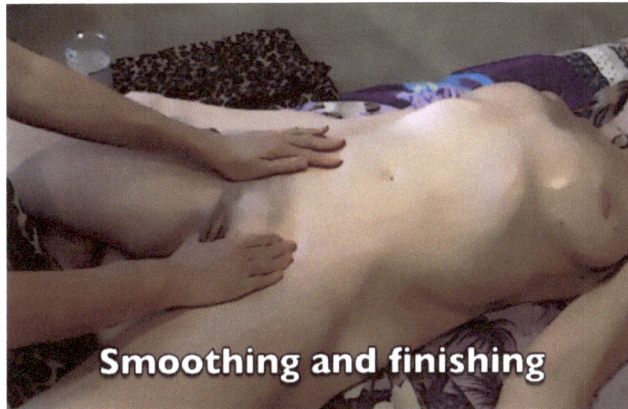

Smoothing and finishing

Do **bladder release**, groin **lymph drain** and **inguinal ligament** moves. Then smoothing and flowing strokes to the torso

Slowly Apply oil to yoni

Ask if you can work on the yoni. The slower you apply the oil to the yoni the better. Move at a snails pace for more relaxation

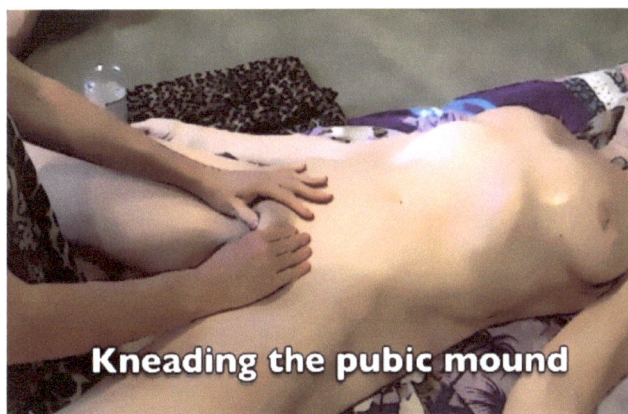

Kneading the pubic mound

Pull and knead the pubic mound

Stretching the Mound
releasing the clitoris

Grasp the tissue of the pubic mound firmly and stretch it toward the head with your thumbs under it

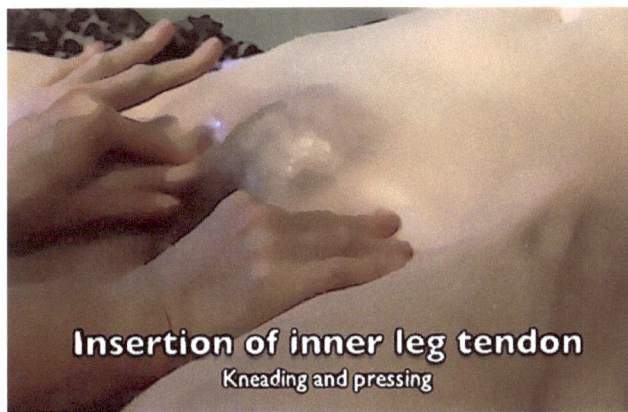

Insertion of inner leg tendon
Kneading and pressing

Massage on both sides of the insertion of the inner thigh tendon where it attaches to the pubic bone

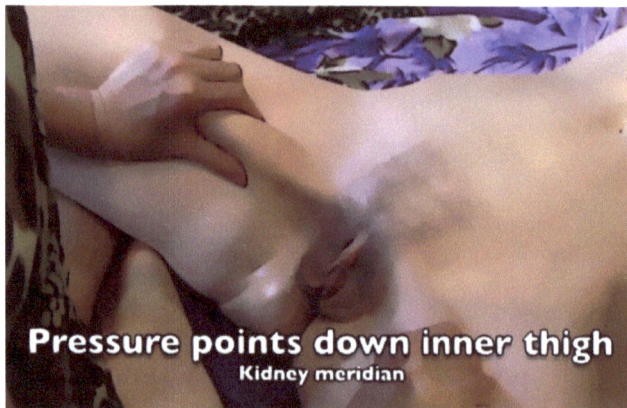

Pressure points down inner thigh
Kidney meridian

Deep pressure and strokes on the line of points from the pubic bone down the inner thigh

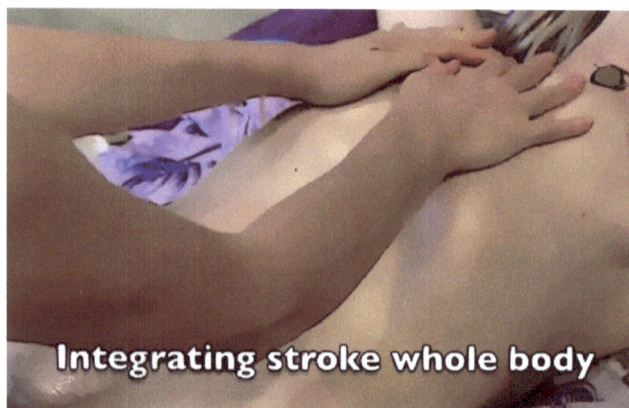

Integrating stroke whole body

Then long smooth strokes to integrate.

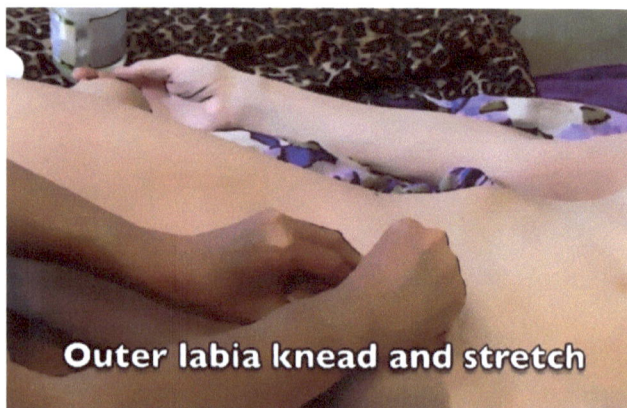

Outer labia knead and stretch

Pick up the outer labia and pull, stretch and roll them between your fingers

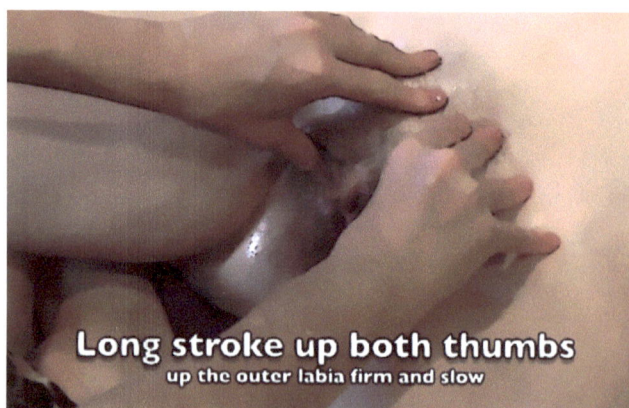

Long stroke up both thumbs
up the outer labia firm and slow

Pressing with both thumbs, make a long slow stroke up both outer labia. this stimulates the legs of the clitoris

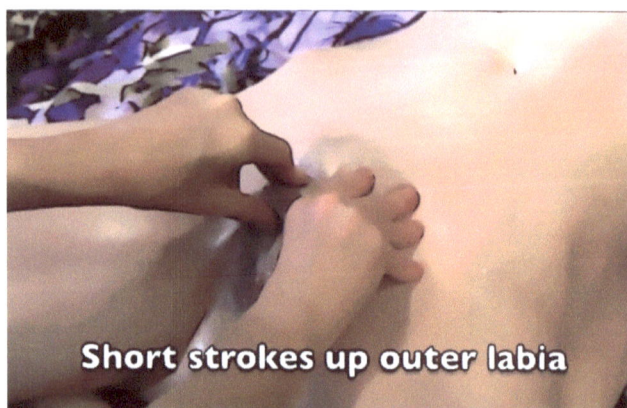

Short strokes up outer labia

Massage and circles on the outer labia

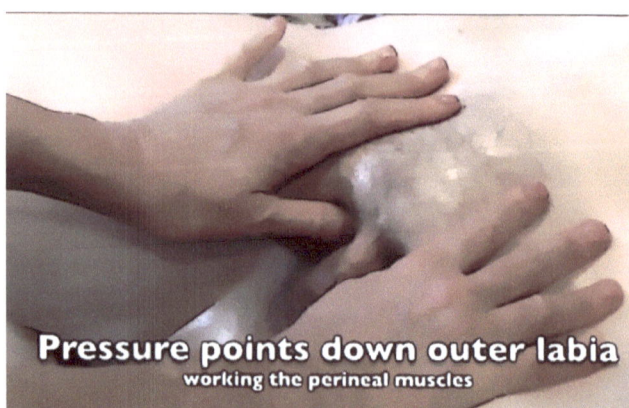

Pressure points down outer labia
working the perineal muscles

Deep pressure on the line of points from either side of the clitoris to the sides of the vagina

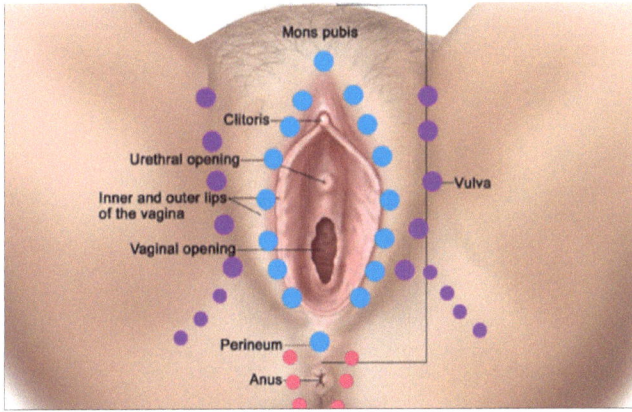

The line of pressure points on the yoni and perineum.

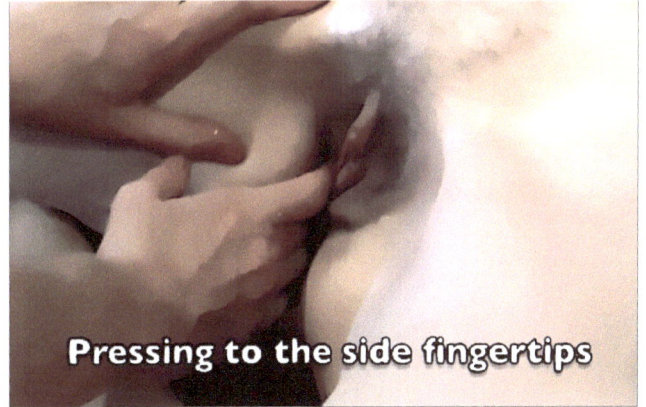

Pressing to the side fingertips

Deep pressure circles on the perineum to the sides of the vagina. Feel the sits bone and curl under and inside it

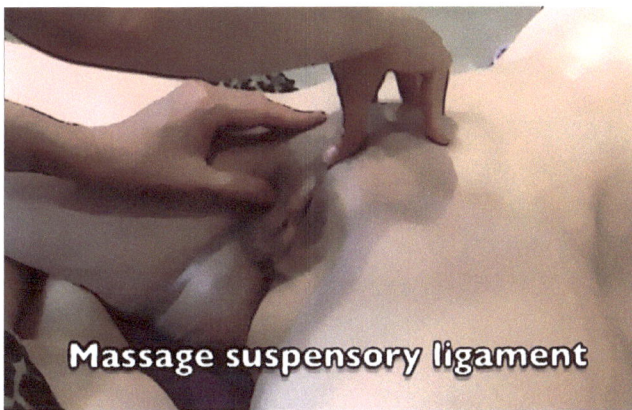

Massage suspensory ligament

Massage the suspensory ligament above the clitoris for some indirect arousal

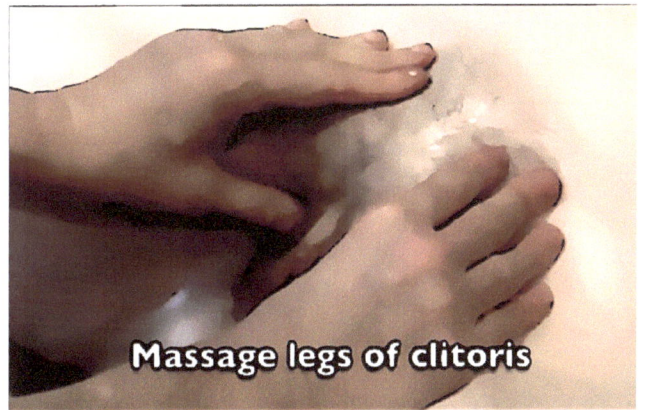

Massage legs of clitoris

Massage down the legs of the clit, along the boney ridge

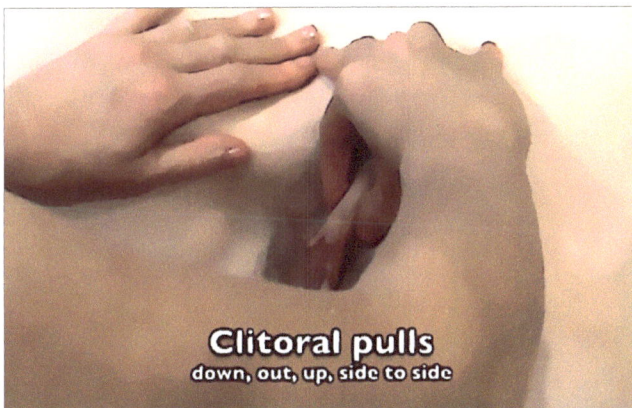

Clitoral pulls
down, out, up, side to side

Grasp underneath the clit thumb and forefinger firmly, and pull it slowly down, up, side to side, and away from the body

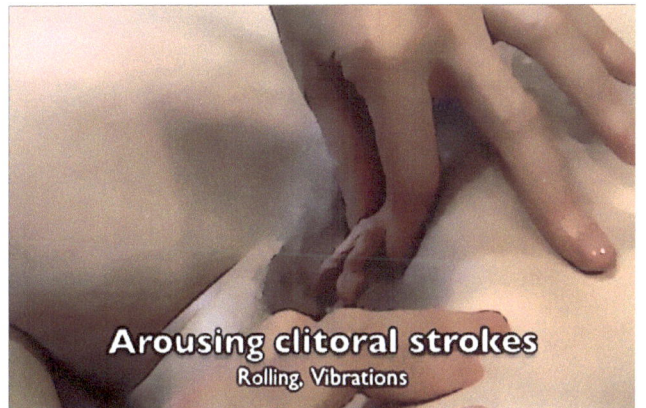

Arousing clitoral strokes
Rolling, Vibrations

Roll and vibrate the shaft of the clit between your fingers to build arousal

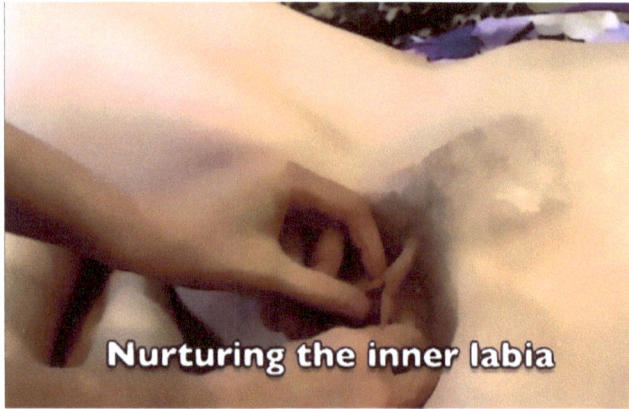

Nurturing the inner labia

Nurture the inner labia with gentle pulls and rolling between your fingers

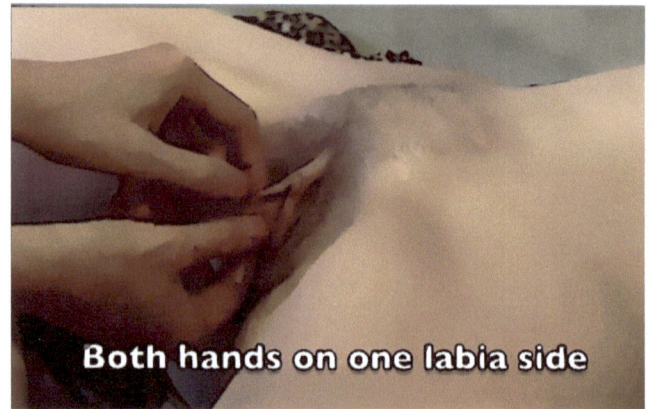

Both hands on one labia side

Use both hands to pull and roll one inner labia slowly and gently, one at a time, all the way down it

Stroke between inner & outer labia

Stroke up and down between the inner and outer labia

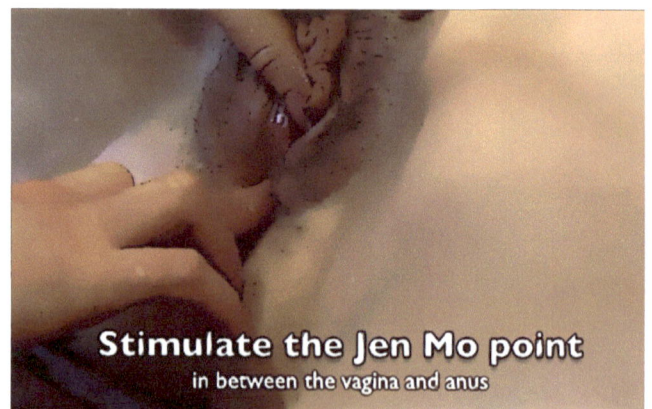

Stimulate the Jen Mo point
in between the vagina and anus

Press in circles on the perineum point between vagina and anus, to stimulate the Jen Mo point

Stroking the power pearl

Roll, stroke and pull on the clitoral tip if she is ready for that arousal. Good arousal is needed to enter the vagina

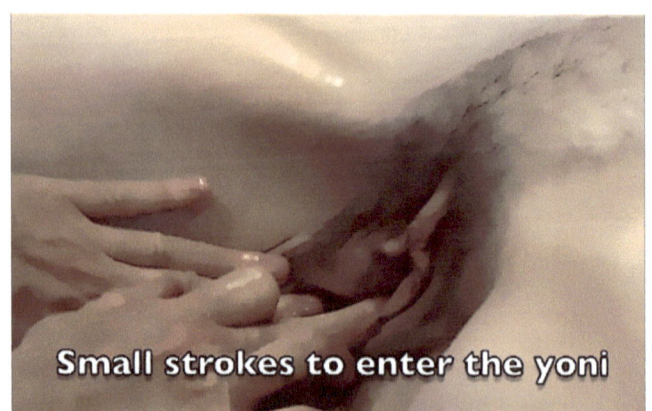

Small strokes to enter the yoni

Ask if she wants you to enter the vagina, and begin small outward strokes around the entrance

Circle around the entrance

Do a slow sweep around the vaginal entrance about one knuckle deep, pressing gently to the outside

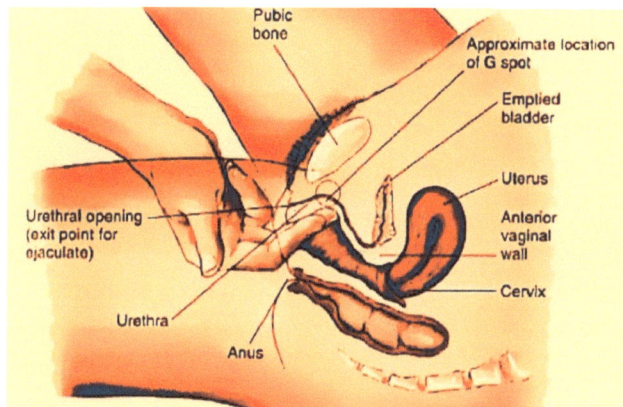

Work your way in deeper with slow strokes. Find the G spot on the top

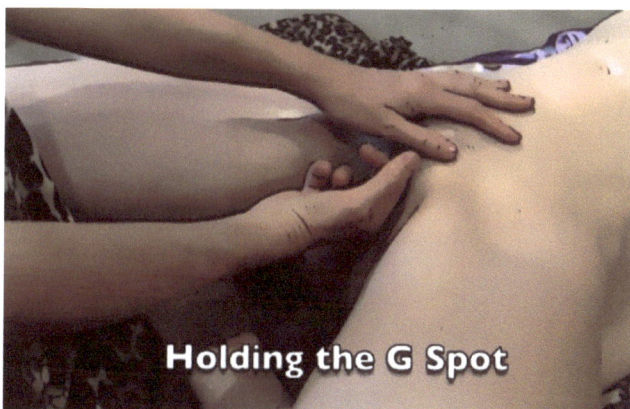

Holding the G Spot

Hold the G spot with steady gentle pressure and your other hand on the pubic mound. Imagine running energy between them

Circling the G spot

Circle around the small bumpy area of the Goddess spot and find its edges. Stroke it by curling your finger. Vibrate it

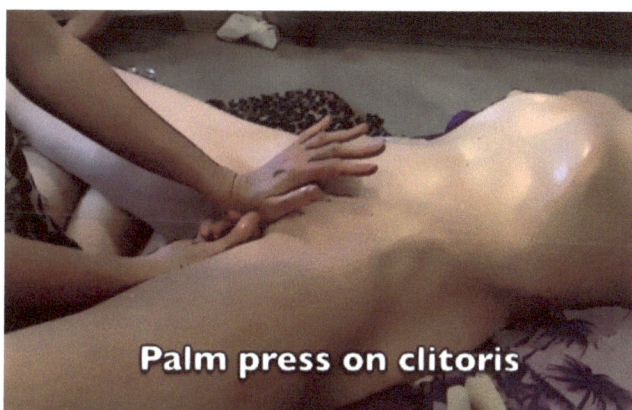

Palm press on clitoris

Press your palm firmly on the clit while working inside for more arousal. Circle the palm

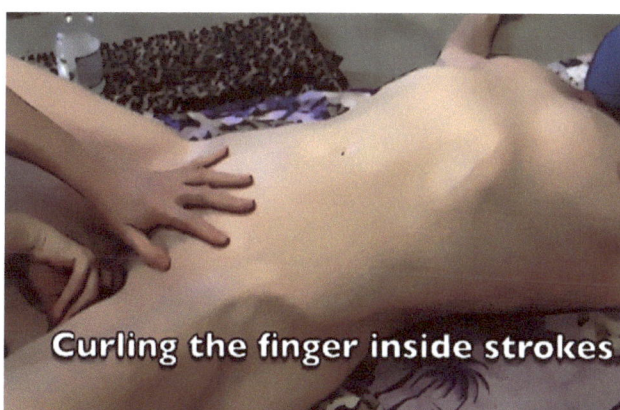

Curling the finger inside strokes

Work around all the areas of the vagina with strokes pressing and curling your finger, and pulling from inside out

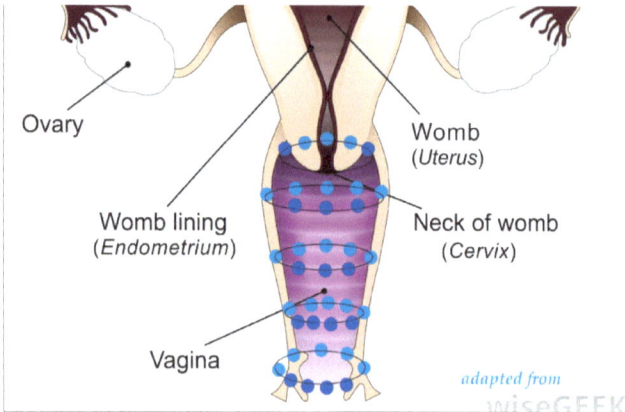

Ovary
Womb (*Uterus*)
Womb lining (*Endometrium*)
Neck of womb (*Cervix*)
Vagina

adapted from wiseGEEK

Deep pressure on the points inside the vagina, at different depths. Notice which points are sore, numb or arousing

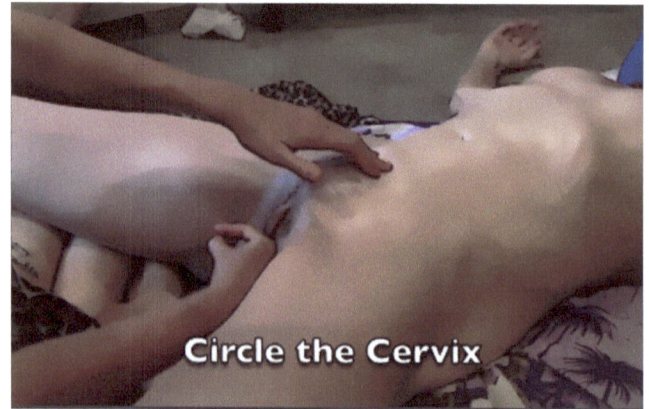

Circle the Cervix

Find the cervix at the very back and circle around it. Press and stimulate the point just in front of it or just behind

Sweep around the clock

Keeping a firm pressure with your fingertip into the vaginal wall, turn your wrist to make sweeps at different depths

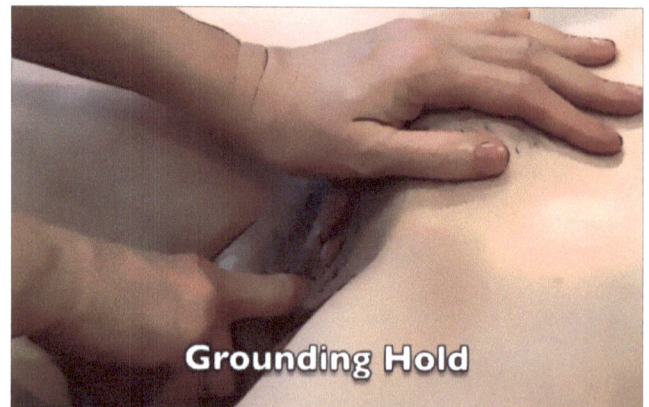

Grounding Hold

With finger inserted facing downward, press on perineal sponge and hold it and breathe. Massage the inside of sacrum

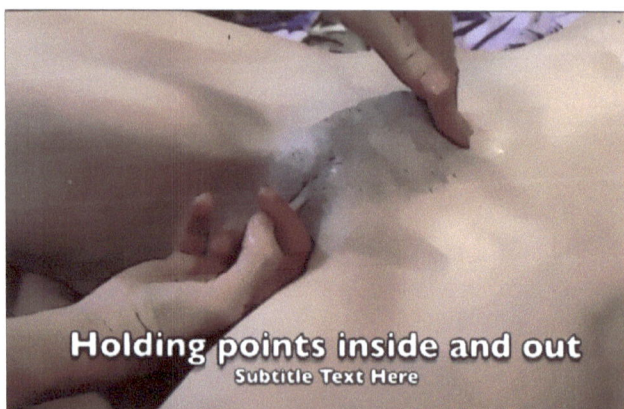

Holding points inside and out
Subtitle Text Here

Points inside the vagina that need release can be held with steady pressure or vibration, while holding external points

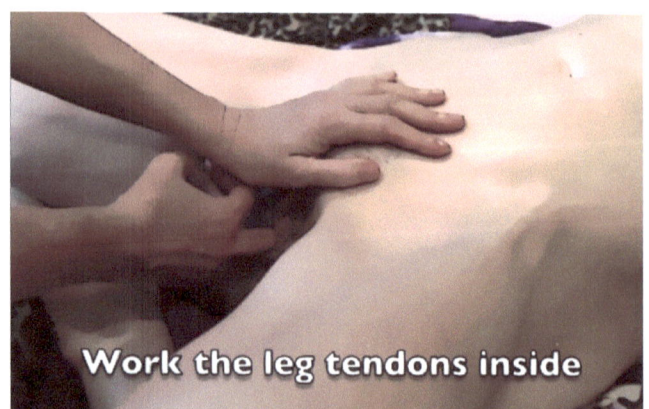

Work the leg tendons inside

The tendons of the thigh can be massaged from inside the vagina

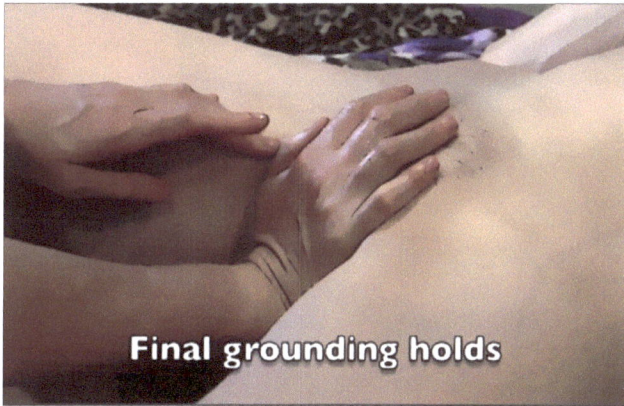

Final grounding holds

After slowly pulling out, press your palm against the entire yoni very firmly and hold

Squeeze PC muscles draw energy up

Ask her to squeeze her pelvic floor muscles and inhale, to bring the energy up and all around the body

Roll to one side

Do some full body integration strokes, and press on the feet.

Help her roll to one side and curl up

Finish with spooning

Lay down behind her and spoon while she relaxes and integrates.

After a few minutes, ask her if there is anything she would like to share about how she is feeling.

Share some things that you appreciate about her.

Take a break. Take time to rest, sleep or meditate.

If you wish to make love, take a break for a while and then come back.

It is best to let the healing session be a separate event from lovemaking.

Front Side Belly and Lingam Massage

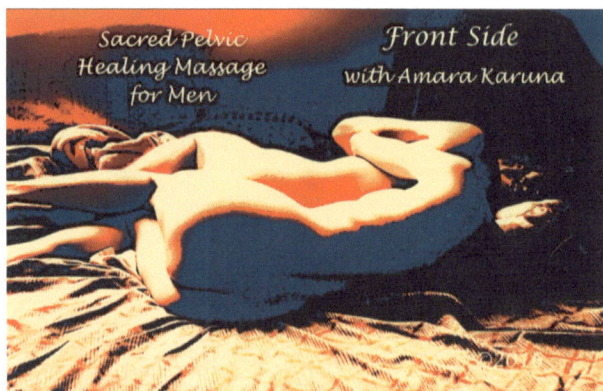

Sacred Pelvic Healing Massage for Men

Front Side with Amara Karuna

After you do the back side massage, turn over. Work with a man first around the lingam, and then spread the energy to other

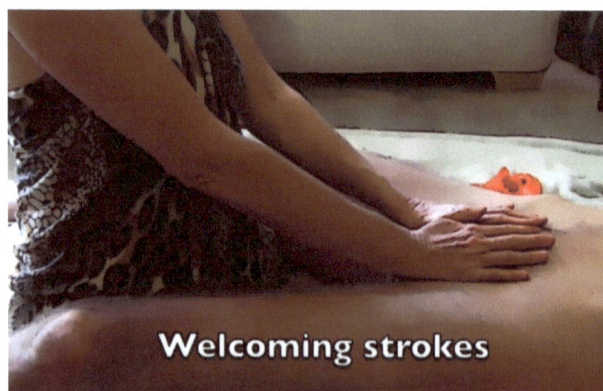

Welcoming strokes

Sit between his legs or on the side. Do some light, slow strokes over the whole body

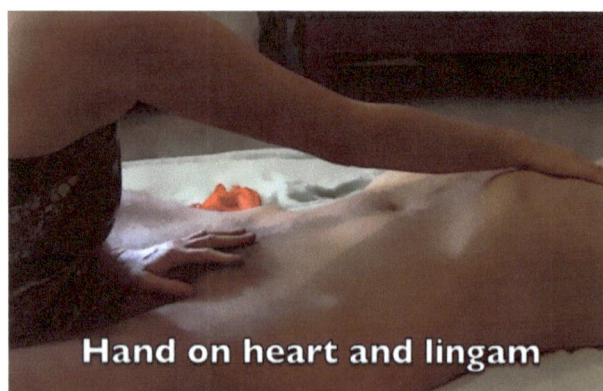

Hand on heart and lingam

Take a moment to look in his eyes, breathe and connect, after you ask permission to hold his lingam and heart

Apply oil slowly around lingam

Apply oil sensually to the lingam, thighs and belly

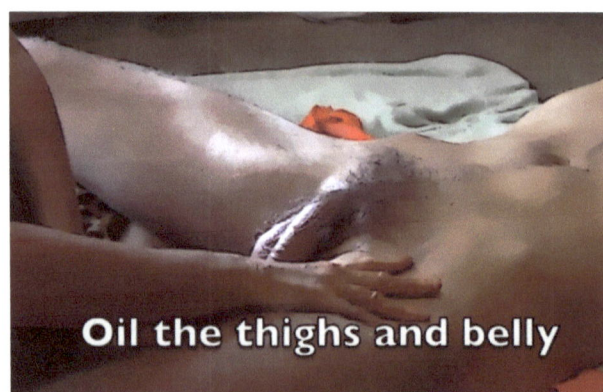

Oil the thighs and belly

Use enough oil so that the hair will not be pulled. Not so much on the lingam yet.

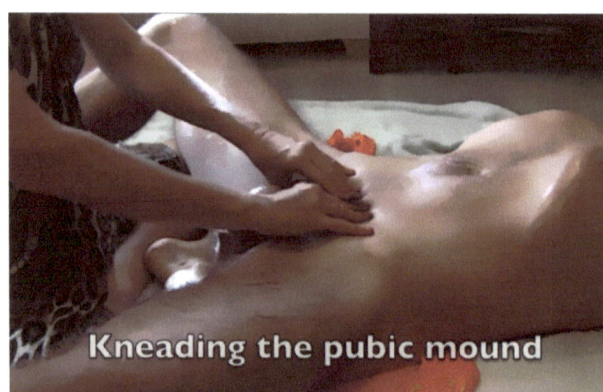

Kneading the pubic mound

Knead the soft hairy area of the pubic mound firmly

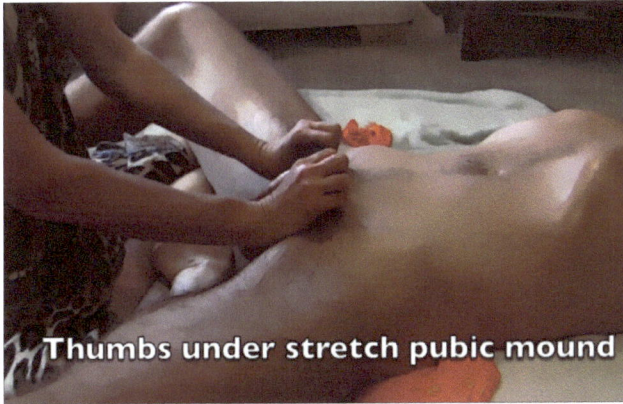
Thumbs under stretch pubic mound

Stretch the facia of the pubic mound with thumbs underneath pulling toward head

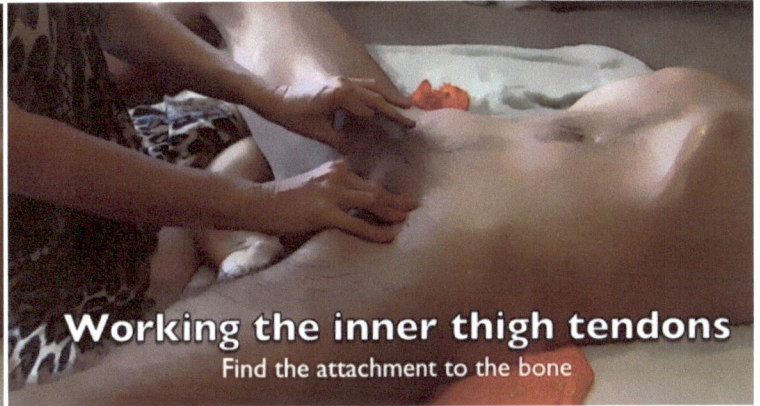
Working the inner thigh tendons
Find the attachment to the bone

Massage the connection of the inner thigh muscles tendon and the pubic bone

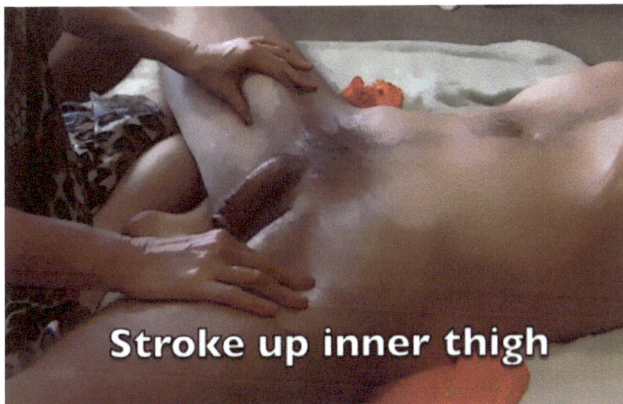
Stroke up inner thigh

Stroke up the inner thigh muscles and work the pressure points there

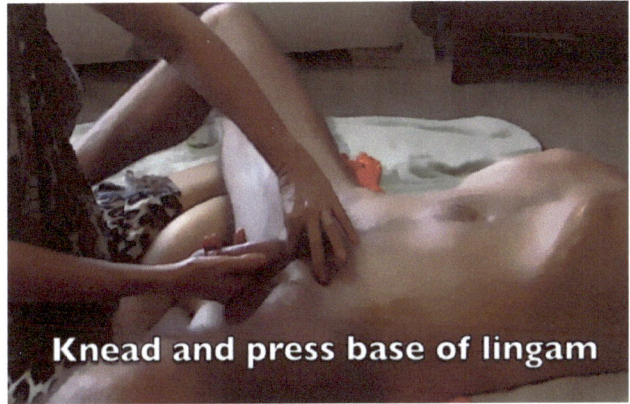
Knead and press base of lingam

Find the place where the lingam attaches to the torso and knead and press around it

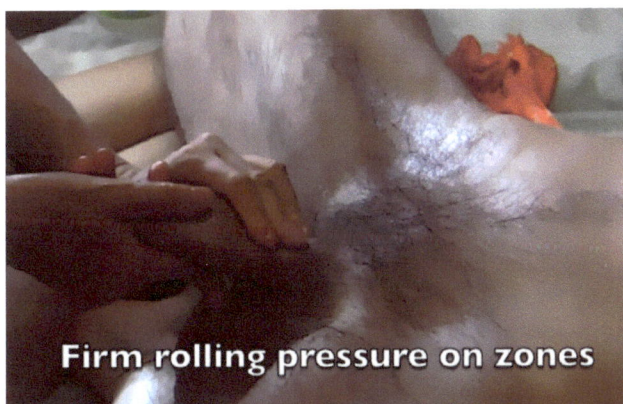
Firm rolling pressure on zones

Use firm pressure and rolling movements on all the reflex zones of the lingam

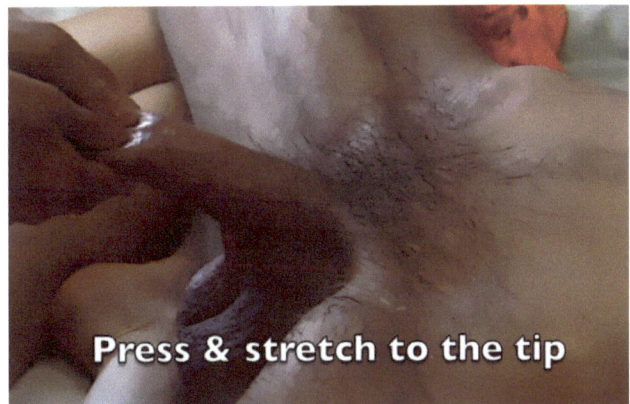
Press & stretch to the tip

Press deeply and stretch the lingam all the way to the tip. You can also grasp the lingam firmly an pull it up, down, to sides

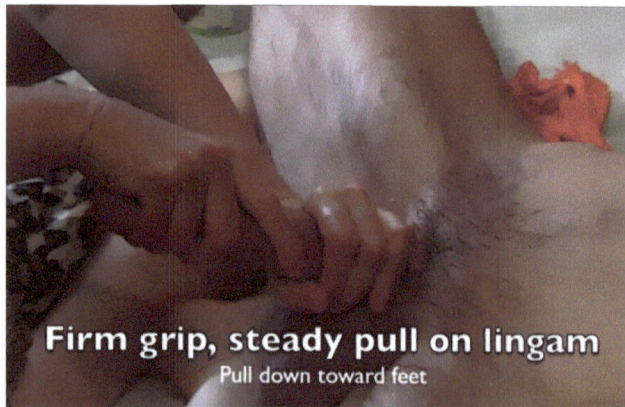

Firm grip, steady pull on lingam
Pull down toward feet

Get a firm grip on the base of the lingam to pull it away from the body, with a long steady pull

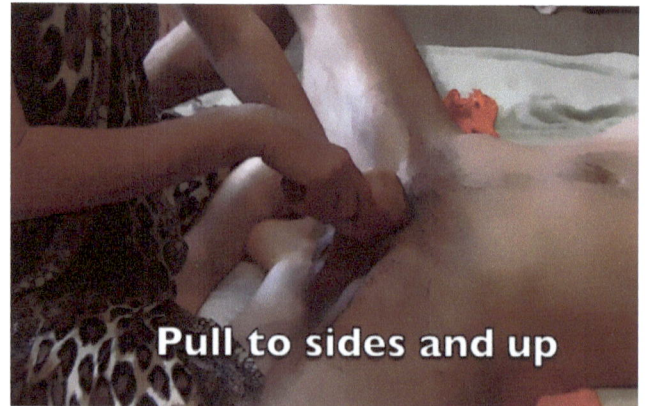

Pull to sides and up

Maintaining the firm grip and pressure, stretch it to each side

Stroke up thigh to groin with pull

While stretching to side, use your other hand to stroke up the inside of the opposite thigh

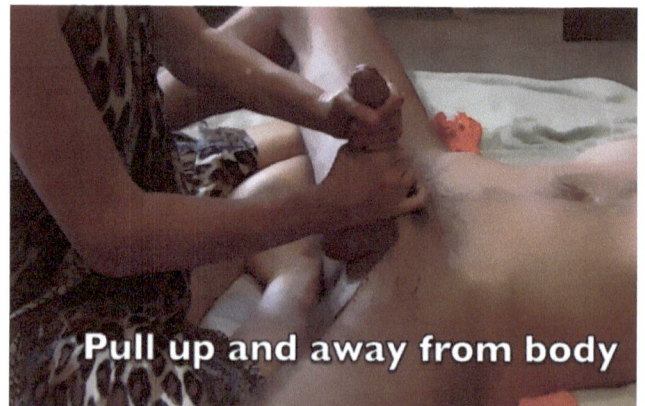

Pull up and away from body

Maintaining the firm grip and pressure, stretch it up and away from the torso

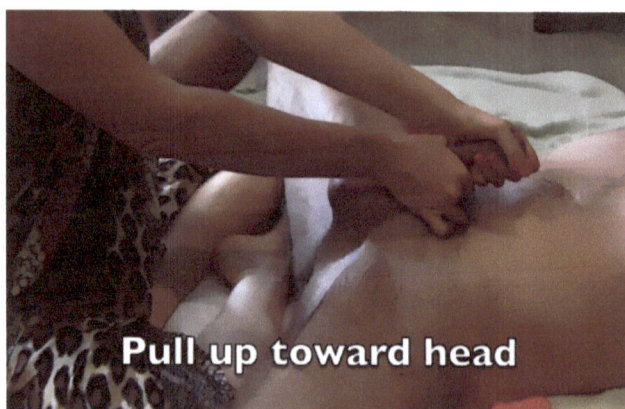

Pull up toward head

Maintaining the firm grip and pressure, stretch it tup toward the head

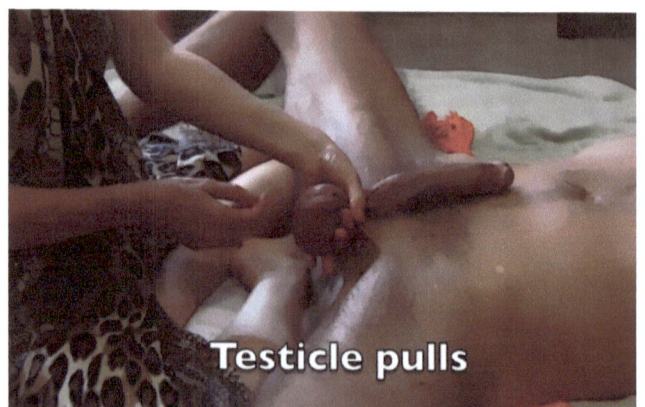

Testicle pulls

Release the lingam and find a firm grip around the base of the testicles, careful to squeeze above them

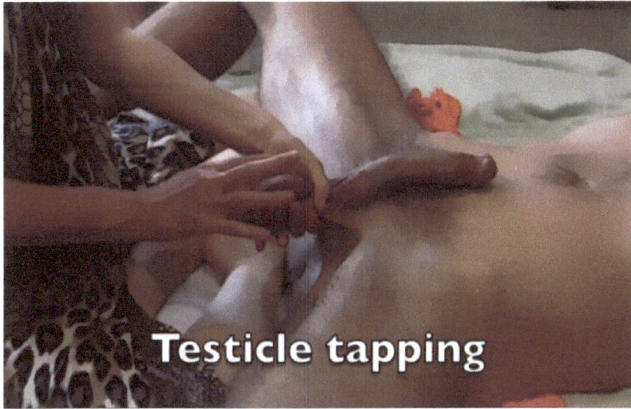
Testicle tapping

Grasp the scrotum in a firm grip above the testicles, and lightly tap them. No testicle pressure

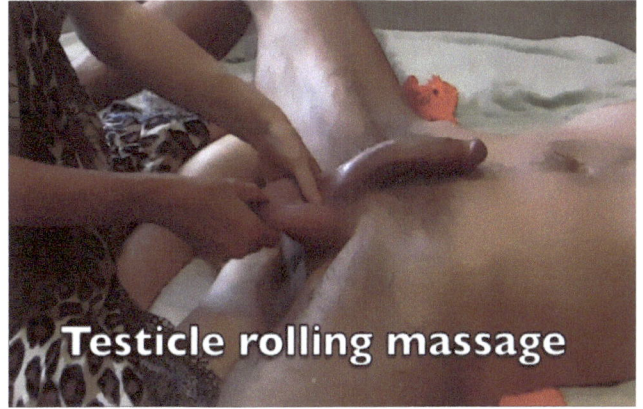
Testicle rolling massage

Roll the testicles around in the scrotum gently between your fingers

Scrotum pulls

Pull on the loose skin of the scrotum gently.

You might do **stretches of the lingam** here. grasp the base firmly, pull up, down, to sides

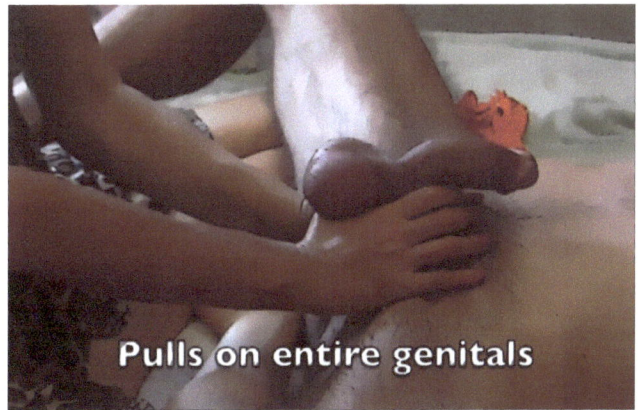
Pulls on entire genitals

Grasp firmly under testicles and around lingam. Pull with steady pressure to stretch the facia deep into the torso

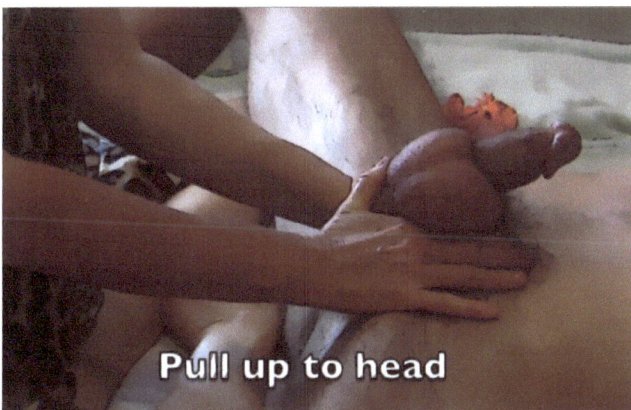
Pull up to head

Pull up towards the head of body. Be sure you are gripping under the testicles not on them. It is a tight grip to avoid slipping

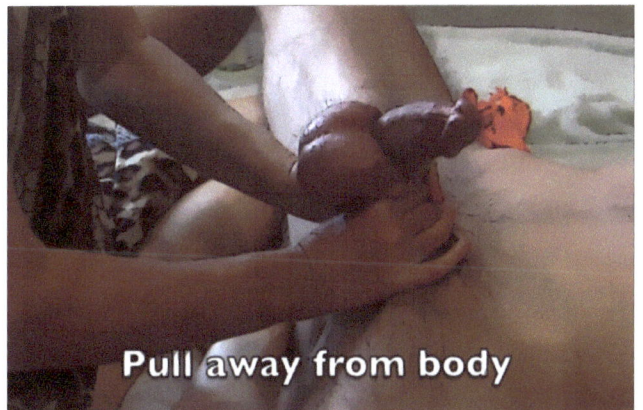
Pull away from body

Pull out and away from the body. No, it does not hurt him!

Pull to sides

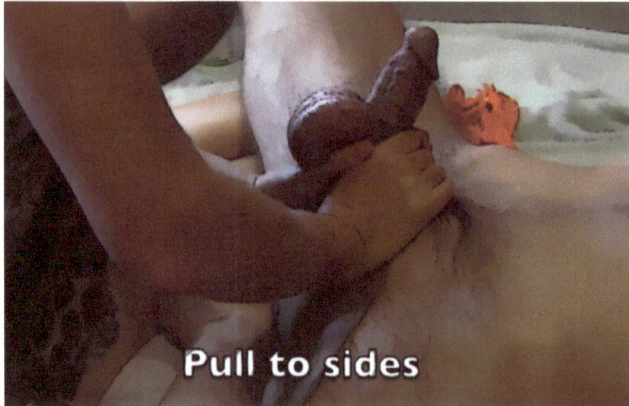

Pull with steady pressure to the sides. Remind him to breathe

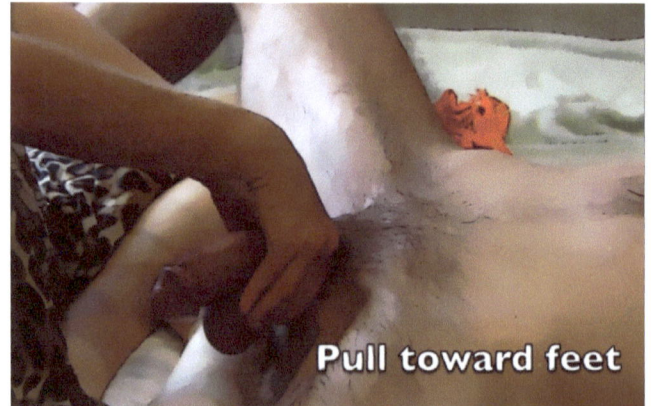

Pull toward feet

Pull with steady pressure towards the feet

Spreading the energy

Release the grasp and do spreading strokes around the entire area

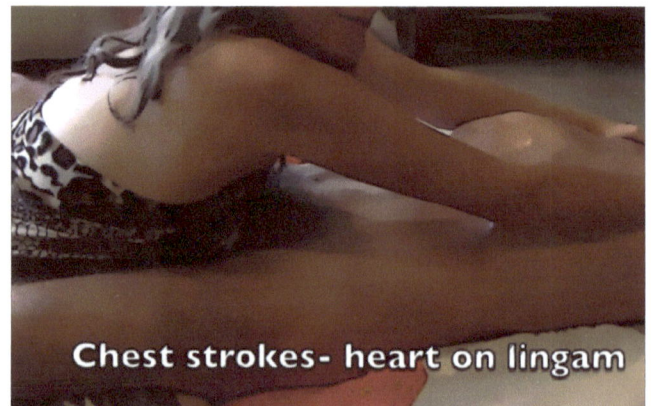

Chest strokes- heart on lingam

Spread the strokes up to the chest and nipples. This makes a moment for your heart to be on his lingam

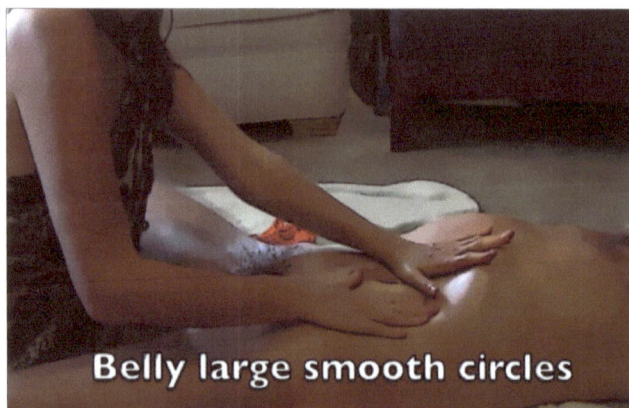

Belly large smooth circles

Focus on the belly in large smooth circles with flat hands.

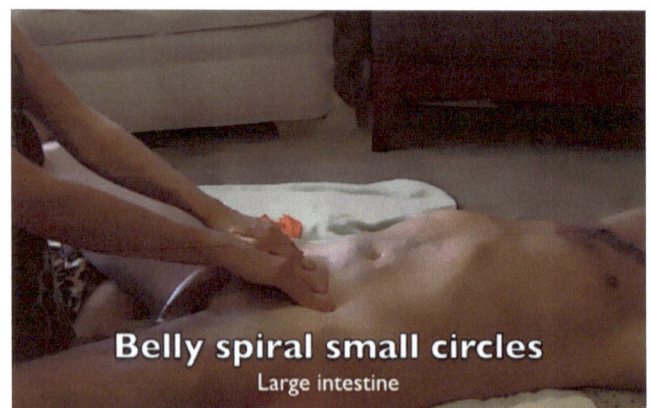

Belly spiral small circles
Large intestine

Move in a clockwise spiral making small circles on the large intestine

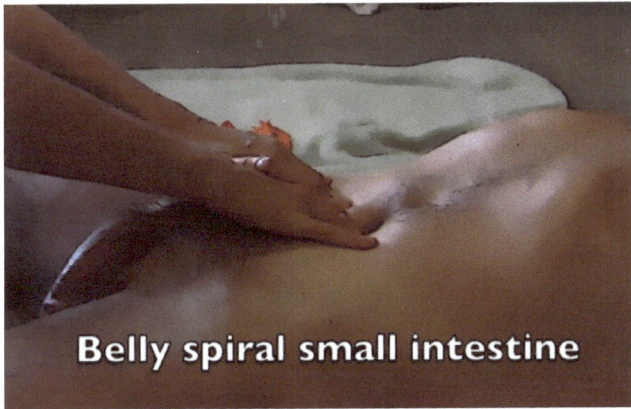

Belly spiral small intestine

Move in a clockwise smaller spiral making small circles on the small intestine

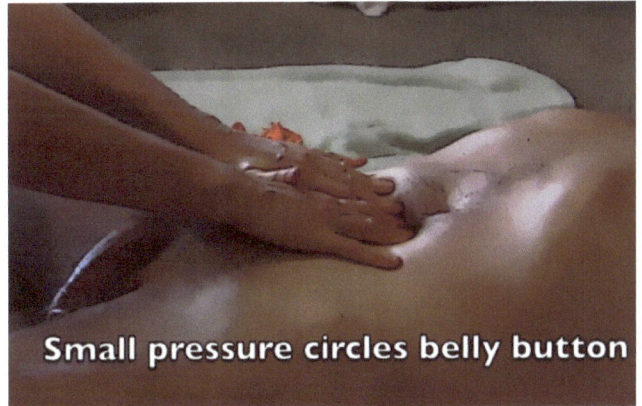

Small pressure circles belly button

Pressing deeply a half inch from the belly button, move in a clockwise circle making small circles all around it

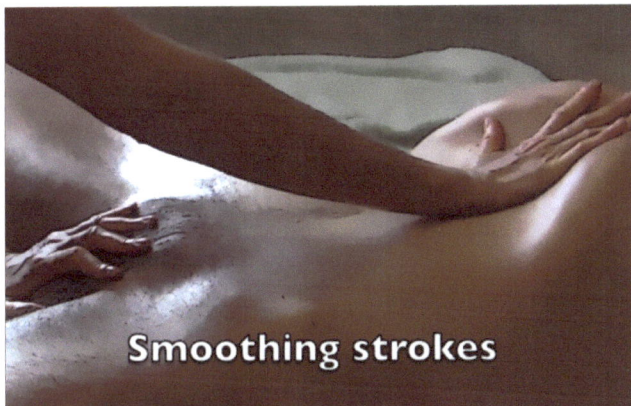

Smoothing strokes

Smooth the whole belly. Then with a broad flat hand, lean in from one side to **press the whole belly to the other side**. Repeat from other direction

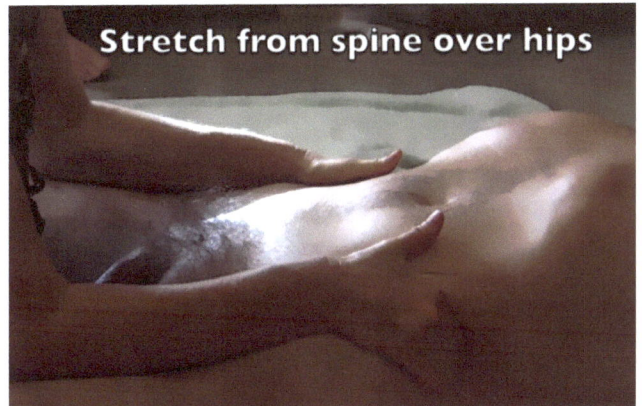

Stretch from spine over hips

Reaching under to touch the spine with your fingertips, press up firmly and sweep up around sides, over hips, to pubic bone

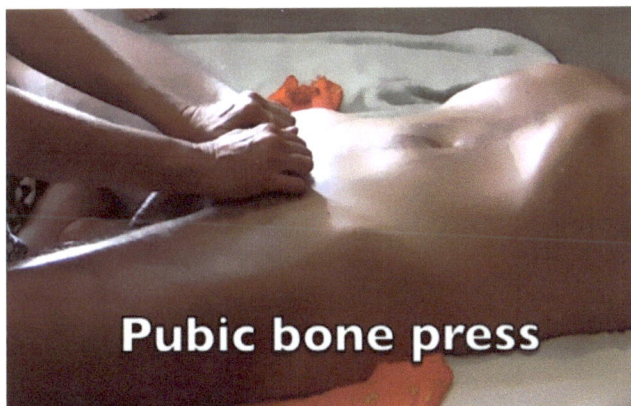

Pubic bone press

At the end of the sweep, press on the pubic bone

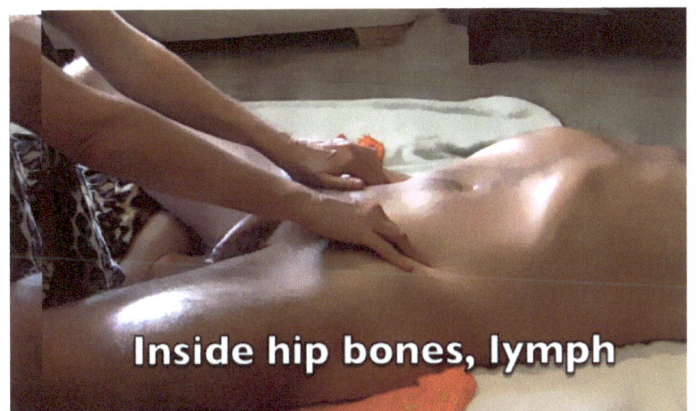

Inside hip bones, lymph

Massage inside the hip bones, and stroke downward to drain the lymph

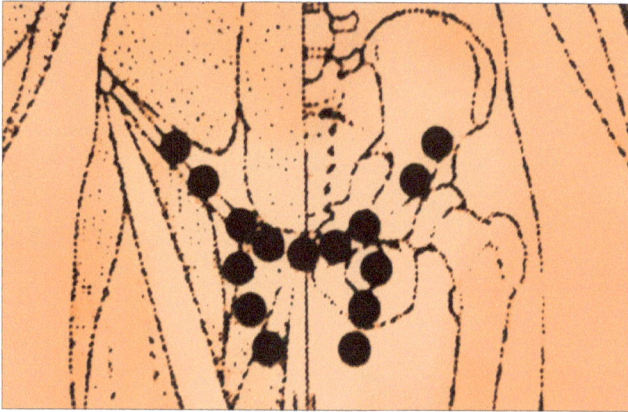

Acupressure points on groin and thighs

Image from Acupressure for Lovers

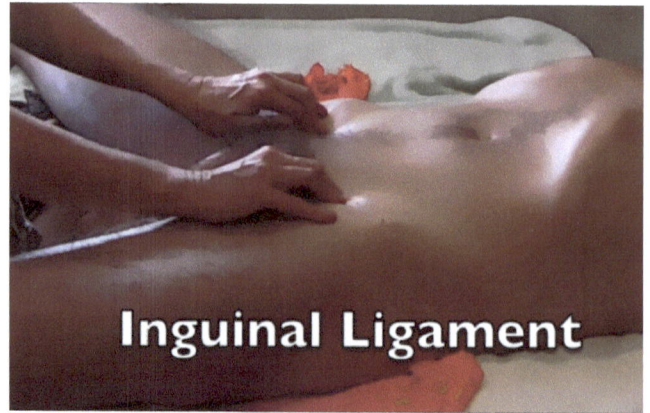

Inguinal Ligament

Massage ropey ligament between the legs and groin, where many pressure points are located

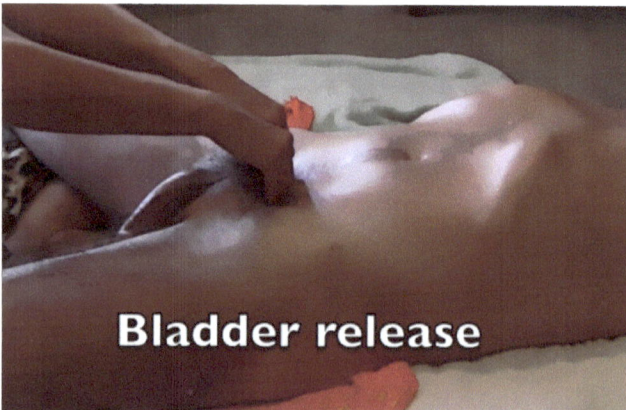

Bladder release

With all fingers straight, press slowly and firmly above public bone and curl under it. Hold for a couple breaths

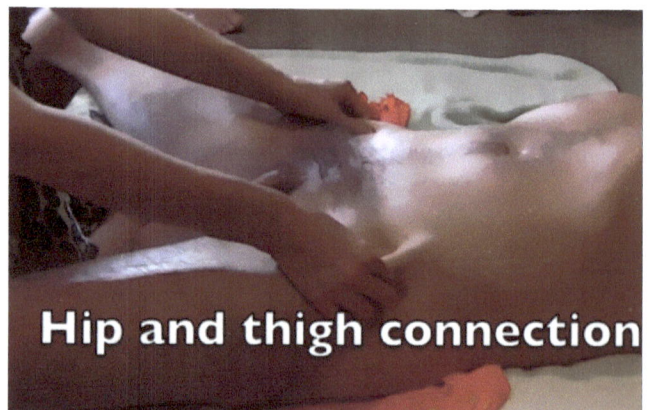

Hip and thigh connection

Massage the insertion of the upper thigh muscle into the torso

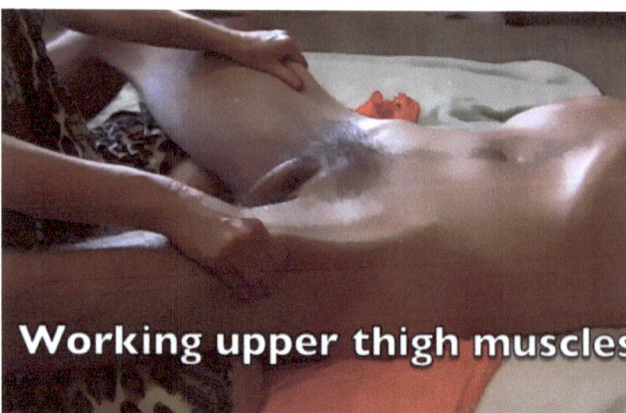

Working upper thigh muscles

Massage down the upper thigh muscle group on the front of the leg

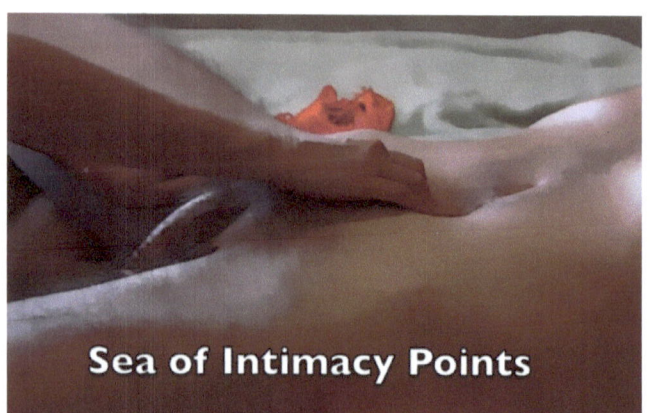

Sea of Intimacy Points

Deep pressure and small circles down the line of points between the belly button and pubic bone

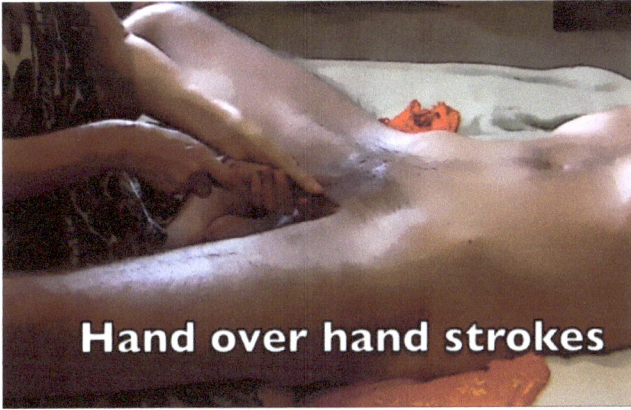

Hand over hand strokes

AROUSING STROKES- Ask if he is ready for some arousal. Pull slowly on lingam alternating hands

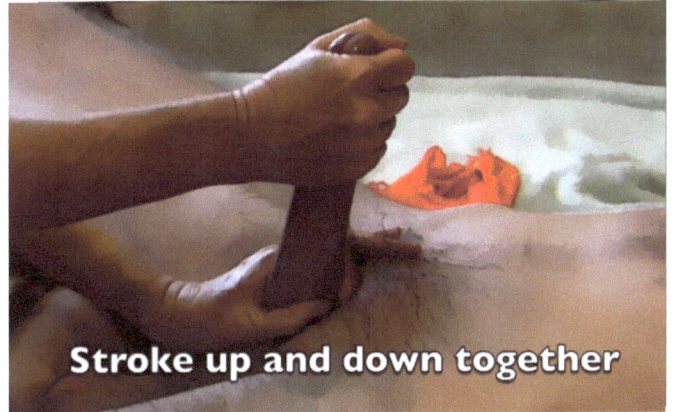

Stroke up and down together

Beginning in the middle, move one hand up the shaft and the other hand down to base

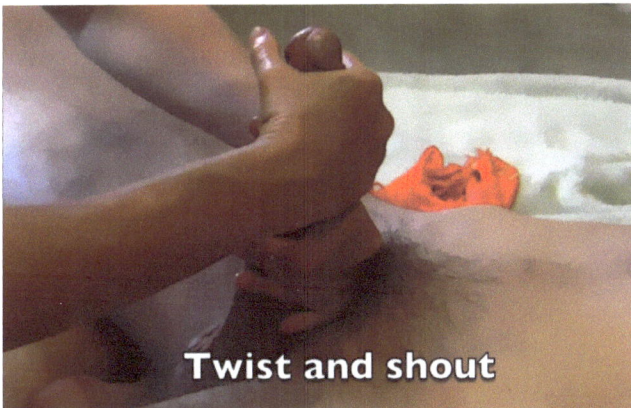

Twist and shout

Surround the shaft with both hands, and twist in opposite directions, gentle but firm

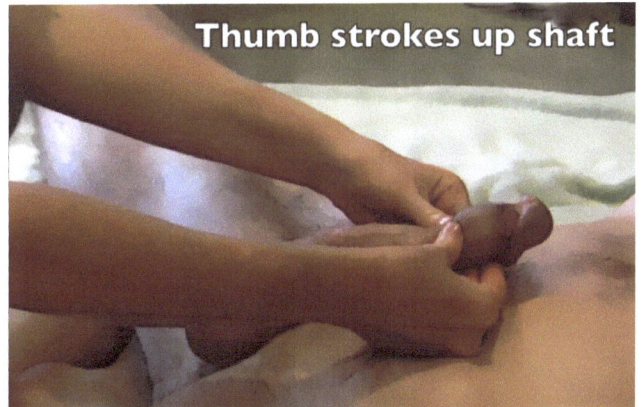

Thumb strokes up shaft

Do a slow steady stroke up the bottom of shaft with both thumbs

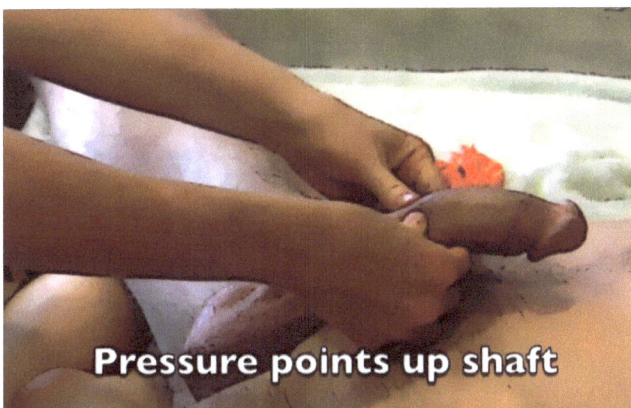

Pressure points up shaft

Deep pressure points up the bottom of the shaft, and rolling between thumb and fingers

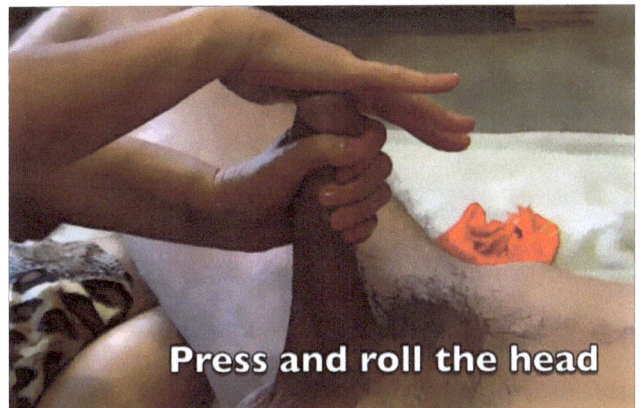

Press and roll the head

Holding the shaft in one hand, press with palm of other hand on the head with a slow rolling movement

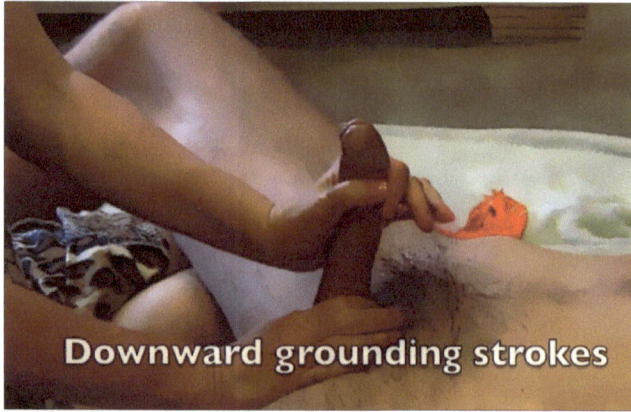

Downward grounding strokes

Stroke firmly down the shaft for grounding the energy

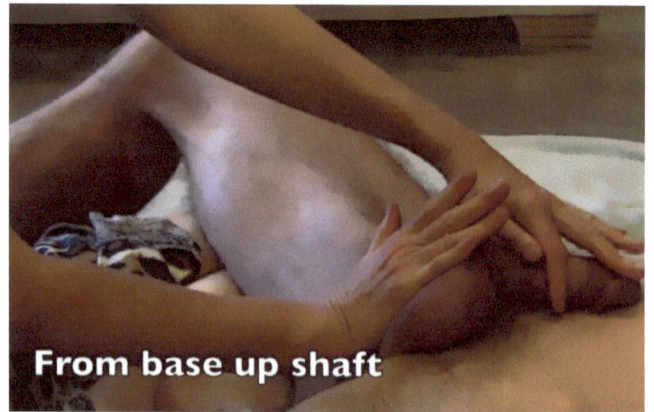

From base up shaft

Press one palm on root of lingam, and stroke firm and slow between testicles up the shaft. No testicle pressure

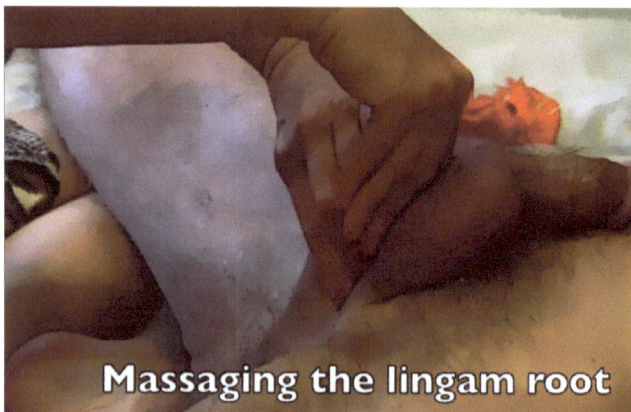

Massaging the lingam root

Massage all around the root of the lingam, under the testicles

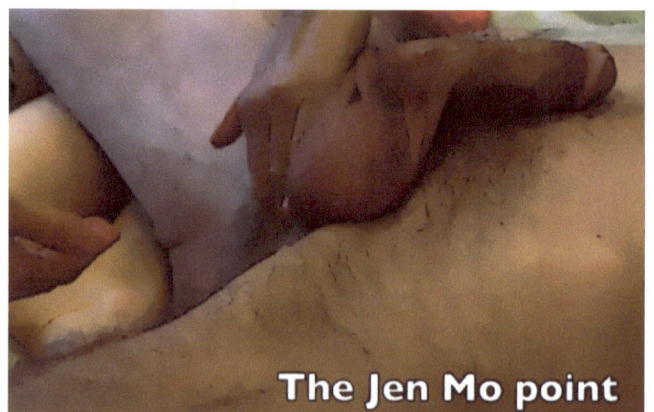

The Jen Mo point

Press with wide pressure on the Jen Mo CV1 point on the perineum, at the base of the lingam root

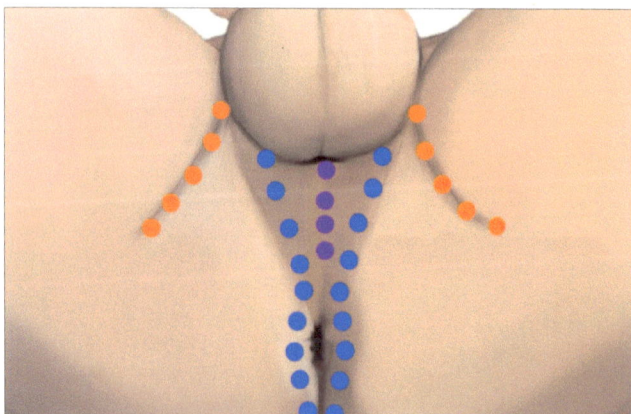

Pressure point lines on the male perineum

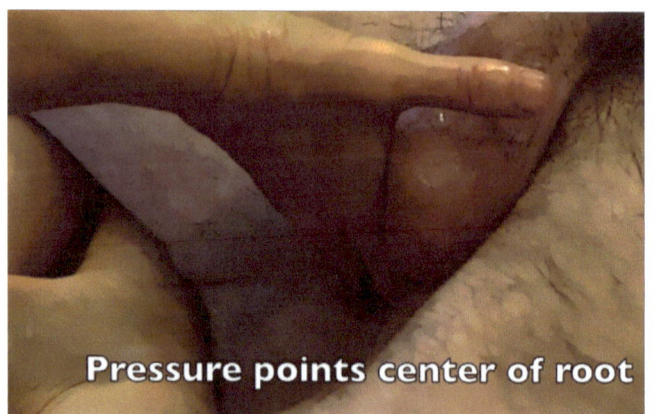

Pressure points center of root

Deep pressure and small circles down the center line between testicles and anus

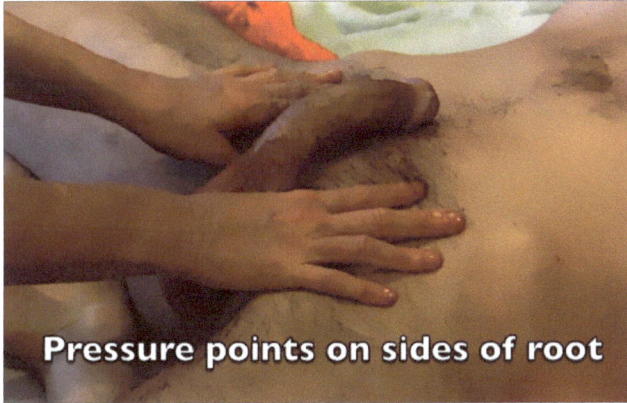

Pressure points on sides of root

Deep pressure and small circles down the lines on the sides of the root. Feel for the sits bones

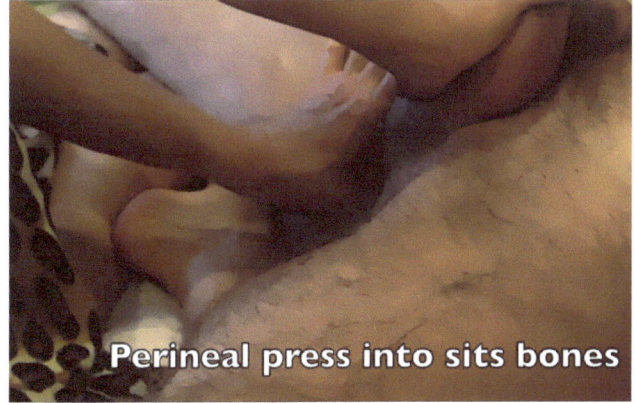

Perineal press into sits bones

Feel for the sits bones and curl your thumbs under and inside them, moving slowly

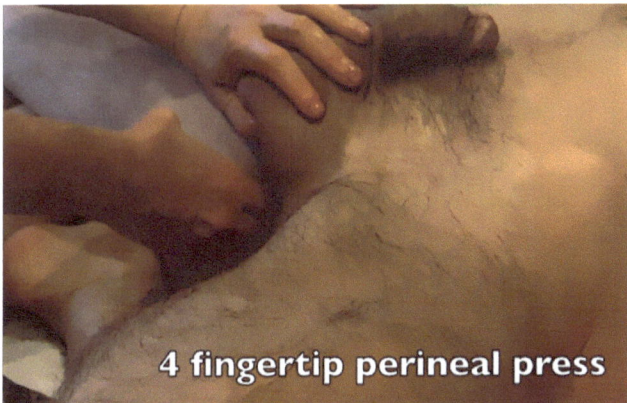

4 fingertip perineal press

Feel for the sits bones and curl your fingers under and inside them, moving slowly from the opposite side

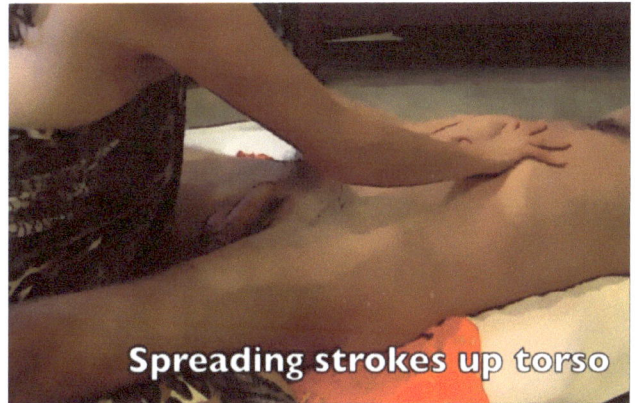

Spreading strokes up torso

Smooth spreading strokes up the torso

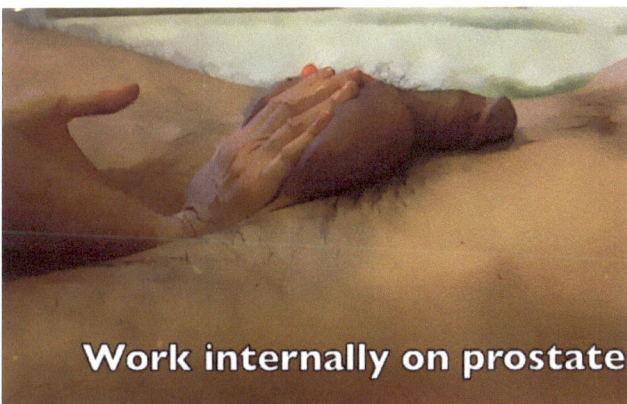

Work internally on prostate

Ask if he wants to have internal prostate massage. If so, do small pressing strokes around the anus to open it

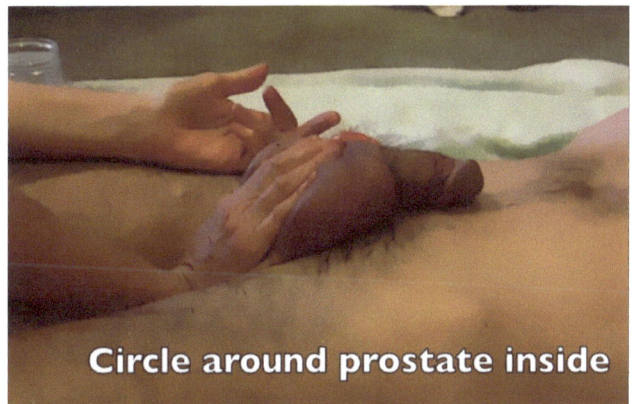

Circle around prostate inside

Gradually moving in deeper, stroke by curling your finger. Find the smooth prostate on top and circle, stroke, vibrate it

Finish hold root and heart

Gradually pull out, wipe fingers, and press firmly with one hand on lingam root, and hold heart with other hand

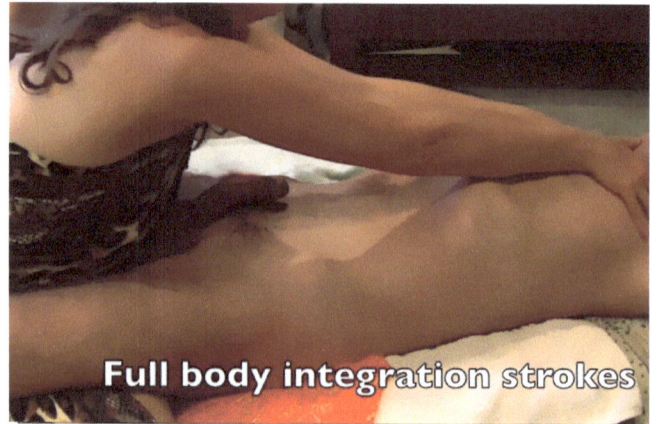
Full body integration strokes

Keep holding the root with the hand that was inside, and stroke the whole body and legs with the other

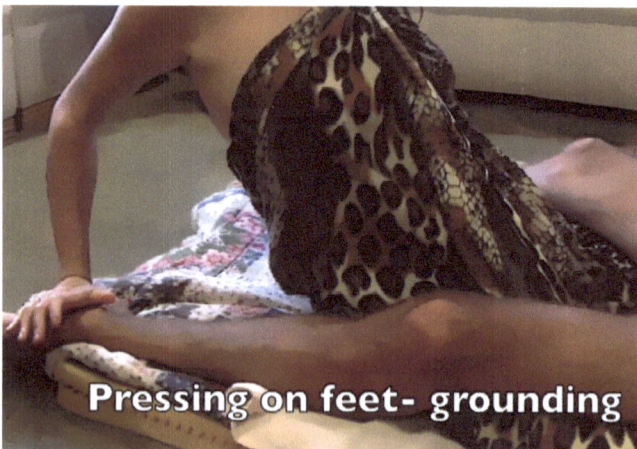
Pressing on feet- grounding

Press and massage down the legs, and press firmly on the feet for grounding

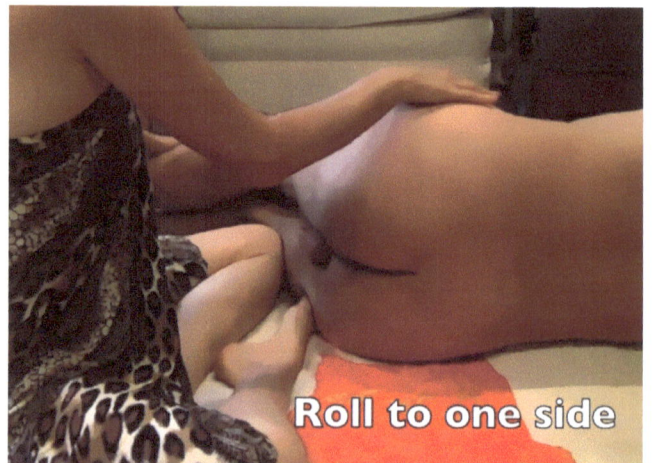
Roll to one side

After a few minutes, ask him if there is anything he would like to share about how he is feeling.

Share some things that you appreciate about him.

Take a break. Take time to rest, sleep or meditate.

If you wish to make love, take a break for a while and then come back.

It is best to let the healing session be a separate event from lovemaking.

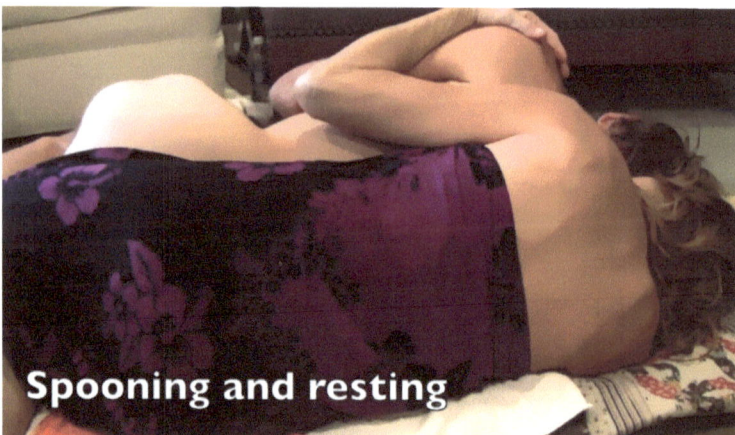
Spooning and resting

Lay behind him spooning and resting for a few minutes.

Recommended Reading
Tantra Recommended Book & DVD list
compiled by Amara Karuna

Books by Amara Karuna, www.karuna-sacredloving.com
The Torus of Life Healing Meditation
Heartbeat Nurturing Therapy: Healing Our Hearts- A Guide for Friends and Lovers

How to Worship the Goddess & Keep Your Balls by David Bruce Leonard

Emergence of the Sensual Woman-Awakening Our Erotic Innocence by Saida Desilets

by Mantak Chia
The Multi-Orgasmic Woman: Sexual Secrets Every Woman Should Know
The Multi-Orgasmic Couple: Sexual Secrets Every Couple Should Know
The Multi-Orgasmic Man: Sexual Secrets Every Man Should Know
Sexual Reflexology: Activating the Taoist Points of Love

Female Ejaculation and the G-Spot by Deborah Sundahl

Tao Tantric Arts for Women by Minke DeVos

Women's Anatomy of Arousal by Sheri Winston

by Margot Anand
The Art of Sexual Ecstasy: The Path of Sacred Sexuality for Western Lovers
The Art of Sexual Magic
Sexual Ecstasy: The Art of Orgasm

by Caroline & Charles Muir
Secrets of Female Sexual Ecstasy DVD
Tantra: The Art of Conscious Loving

by Kamala Devi, Baba Dez Nichols
Sacred Sexual Healing: The SHAMAN Method of Sex Magic

by Micheala Reidl
Lingham Massage- Awakening Male Sexual Energy
and Yoni Massage-Awakening Female Sexual Energy

by Rebecca Chalker- The Clitoral Truth

by Michael Reed Gach- Acupressure for Lovers

About The Author

Amara Karuna has been studying alternative healing since 1978 in many different forms.

In 1989 she developed her own approach to peer counseling, called Holistic Peer Counseling, integrating many ideas from Re-evaluation Co-counseling with spiritual meditation practices, psychic healing, breathwork and body centered techniques.

She has taught hundreds of people to do peer counseling, and has lead many classes and support groups in Hawaii and the west coast, including groups for sexual healing, parents and leaders.

She began studying Tantra and Sacred Spot work, a method of sexual healing, on Maui in 2003, and has since studied six different methods of pelvic bodywork. She has been teaching Sacred Pelvic Healing for men and women, and leading Tantra Pujas since 2007.

She developed **Heartbeat Nurturing Therapy**, a method of healing the inner infant self using cradling, hypnotic induction and suckling to address emotional issues stemming from lack of breast feeding and loving closeness as an infant.

She is the author of **"Heartbeat Nurturing Therapy- Healing Our Hearts Together",** and several other works, as well as several CDs of music.

SEE   http://www.karuna-sacredloving.com

for counseling, classes, workshops, writings, videos

www.ingramcontent.com/pod-product-compliance
Lightning Source LLC
Chambersburg PA
CBHW040916100426
42737CB00042B/100

9 780984 227488